THE SECRET PAINTER

Joe Tucker originally trained as an animation director before becoming a television scriptwriter. With his scriptwriting partner, Lloyd Woolf, he has created and written the BBC shows *Witless*, *Click & Collect* and *Black Ops*.

'*The Secret Painter* is so much more than a sentimental rags to riches yarn. Joe uses his uncle's extraordinary life to tell a broader story about the way that working-class people in the twentieth century were excluded from artmaking.
[A] thoughtful, funny book'
The Times

'A timely reminder that art did not originate as an investment opportunity or a get-rich-quick scheme but as a way for human beings to make sense of their lives (plus make them bearable into the bargain). Miracles happen in the most unlikely places'
JARVIS COCKER

'*The Secret Painter* is a bracingly northern corrective to the metropolitan hype and verbiage that surrounds so much art. Joe Tucker writes with beautiful casualness'
Observer

'A fascinating one-off biography, which lays out the hypocrisy and snobbery of this country's "cultural elite" with an enviable lightness of touch. A book with steel in its heart'
iPaper

'Joe Tucker is a natural storyteller and *The Secret Painter* is a brilliant, engrossing read. His book serves as an important reminder to all of us that the great stories in our lives are often closer to us than we think'
LEMN SISSAY

'A moving account of how the creative imagination can flourish in the most inhospitable circumstances'
Telegraph

'I was hooked from the first couple of pages . . . A lovely read'
ALASTAIR CAMPBELL

'[A] slim but fascinating portrait'
Financial Times

'A thoroughly satisfying enquiry into both a man and an artist. It was such a privilege to experience Eric's world and I loved *The Secret Painter*'
CATHY RENTZENBRINK

'Like his uncle before him, Joe Tucker inserts humanity and humour into the story of art. This is an uplifting, true story behind the many masterpieces found in an attic in Warrington, and how they were finally brought down for the world to see. I couldn't put this joyous book down!'
RUTH MILLINGTON

'[A] beautifully written memoir. Partly out of family fealty and partly out of newfound respect for his uncle's skill and insight, the author doggedly navigates constant twists and turns as he endeavours to get his uncle's paintings catalogued, exhibited and ultimately appreciated'
Library Journal

THE
SECRET
PAINTER

JOE TUCKER

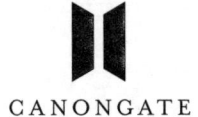

CANONGATE

This paperback edition published in 2025 by Canongate Books

First published in Great Britain in 2025
by Canongate Books Ltd, 14 High Street, Edinburgh EH1 1TE

canongate.co.uk

1

Copyright © Joe Tucker, 2025

All paintings and photographs copyright
© the Estate of Eric Tucker

The right of Joe Tucker to be identified as the
author of this work has been asserted by him in accordance
with the Copyright, Designs and Patents Act 1988

No part of this book may be used or reproduced in any manner for
the purpose of training artificial intelligence technologies or systems.
This work is reserved from text and data mining (Article 4(3) Directive
(EU) 2019/790)

British Library Cataloguing-in-Publication Data
A catalogue record for this book is available on
request from the British Library

ISBN 978 1 83726 080 5

Typeset in Garamond MT Std by Palimpsest Book Production Ltd,
Falkirk, Stirlingshire

Printed and bound by CPI Group (UK) Ltd, Croydon CR0 4YY

The manufacturer's authorised representative in the EU for product
safety is Authorised Rep Compliance Ltd, 71 Lower Baggot Street,
Dublin D02 P593 Ireland
(www.arccompliance.com)

For my family and for Eric

'There are moments when Art attains almost to the dignity of manual labour.'
From 'The Model Millionaire' by Oscar Wilde

CONTENTS

1. A Portrait of the Artist as an Old Man ... 1
2. Would the Man from the *New York Times* Like Some Sandwiches? ... 8
3. Uncle Eric ... 22
4. You've Gotta Watch These Buggers ... 37
5. What's Our Eric Doing There? ... 50
6. The Lady in the Photograph ... 69
7. We Need to Talk About Norman ... 89
8. I'm Not Good Enough Yet ... 103
9. The Final (Sort of) Wish ... 122
10. The Dreams of Youth ... 138
11. The Other Eric Tucker ... 161
12. Terraced House Tate ... 177

Postscript ... 202
Acknowledgements ... 211

CHAPTER 1

A PORTRAIT OF THE ARTIST AS AN OLD MAN

The only thing that appeared remarkable about my uncle was his dishevelment. And it wasn't a romantic, photogenic dishevelment – like some windswept poet or a fisherman with holes in his cable-knit jumper. It was an emphatically unglamorous, everyday sort of dilapidation. He would shamble arthritically down the terraced streets of his hometown, Warrington, on his daily pilgrimage to Betfred, with his shoelaces undone and an aluminium walking stick tethered to his wrist by string that had been rain-soaked and sun-dried several times over. His personal aesthetic seemed designed to put tramps at ease.

He was a heavyset man, well-built in his youth – a former boxer – around six feet tall but now stooped by old age. He was bald with a ring of lank, grey hair which he occasionally chopped with kitchen scissors. For a time, he used a length of rope as a belt. He had a faded, grey polyester bomber jacket, the pockets a grubby casserole of betting slips, lint and sachets of sugar. He wore it until it began to fall apart at the seams, at which point he patched it back together with Sellotape. This was all partly born out of poverty – but it wasn't simply a matter of necessity. It was, in truth, his preferred look. Try as my parents would to coax him into Marks and

Spencer's Blue Harbour range – with occasional success, it should be said – he would inevitably drift back to what he felt most comfortable in: a moth-nibbled jumper that couldn't have been purchased in that decade or the two preceding it.

It was in the local bookmaker's, at the beginning of my uncle's ninth decade, that Mr Hassan met him. 'He was the only person who would stop and talk to me,' Mr Hassan told me, and I suspect that was reciprocal. Bumping into one another regularly, the two men made small talk and shared horse-racing tips. And over time, a friendship blossomed. Then one day, Mr Hassan realised he wasn't bumping into my uncle quite so often.

By this time, my uncle was finding it increasingly difficult to walk. If there was anything to rouse his powers of mobility, it was a trip to the bookie's. But some days he just couldn't make it – and some days was quickly becoming most days. So Mr Hassan offered to place his bets for him.

Now, accepting such an offer was no small act for my uncle. He was exceptionally mistrustful of most people – including family members – and he generally refused absolutely all offers of help, so obsessed was he with control over his own affairs. But either Mr Hassan had achieved a level of confidence most couldn't, or the draw of gambling was just too strong: my uncle accepted the offer.

Every morning, Mr Hassan would call at his house, where he would come to the front door to hand over his cash and betting slip. And so it went for a while, until my uncle struggled even to make the short walk to his front door. At which point, he started leaving his front door on the latch so Mr Hassan could let himself in.

'That's when I found out about the other part of his life, which he never told me,' Mr Hassan explained.

Coming into my uncle's house for the first time, Mr Hassan made his way to the back room, where my uncle was sitting in his chair, betting slip and cash ready for collection. He passed by the front room, its frosted glass door slightly ajar. Through the gap, a few paintings, propped up against a cabinet, were just about visible. By this time, the pair had been friends for years. Mr Hassan had gotten to know my uncle much better than most. But he had never mentioned anything about painting.

Not long after this, my dad was visiting his older brother – as he did, by then, one or more times a week. By this point, my uncle, increasingly restricted to smaller areas of his house by his limited mobility, largely lived in the one back room. It was an arrangement not helped by his penchant for hoarding.

My uncle had great faith in the idea that almost anything, kept for long enough, would accumulate value. Or at least prove useful. So his sofa was buried under piles of old newspapers and magazines. There were plastic carrier bags you dared not look in, bearing the logos of defunct supermarkets. It was possible, in that room, to lay your hands on small scraps of paper dating from any time in the last half-century. He cooked his meals with a set of pans his mother had won in a competition in the 1960s. And we knew that because a browning newspaper clipping with a picture of my grandmother, the proud new cookware owner, stood on the mantelpiece, alongside three clocks from Argos and countless knick-knacks bought on coach tours.

My uncle was nearing the end of his life. He was in his mid-eighties, he could hardly walk and, crucially, he had a degenerative heart condition for which he was refusing treatment. He knew he was on the way out. And on this particular day, with his younger brother visiting, he tentatively, wistfully ventured that it would have been nice to have had an exhibition of his paintings, at the local museum and art gallery.

Now, my dad knew that his brother liked to paint. We, his family, all did. Between us we had a handful of his pictures hanging on the walls of our homes. A few had been gifted sporadically over the decades. Others had been bought from him – not always easily. But generally, my uncle was highly unforthcoming about his painting activities, even with those close to him. I asked his oldest friend, Alan 'Buller' Crompton, if my uncle had ever talked to him about it. 'He never talked about anything!' Buller replied. 'Eric was a lad who kept himself to himself.'

His mentioning an exhibition was a surprise, in as much as he'd never said anything like it before. In fact, I hadn't even been sure he'd wanted his work to be seen. But there was also something infuriatingly in character about the fact he had only raised it once he believed it was too late. My dad, however, felt that it wasn't too late. That as long as his brother was alive, they might be short on time but they weren't out of it. He suggested they should begin by cataloguing the paintings. My dad would need to understand what work there was. He would need to see it all.

Again, this was no small request to make of my uncle. In later years, he'd grown increasingly possessive and paranoid around his paintings; on tenterhooks if a family member touched or moved one, generally resistant to any perceived infringement on his tight control of them. So in asking to sort through and look at them all, my dad was setting his brother quite the challenge. But to his surprise, his brother agreed.

My dad headed towards the front room – my uncle's painting room, a room we rarely went in – and pushed open the frosted glass door. Inside, there were paintings stacked in rows, covering most of the floor space. One by one, my dad took them out and ferried them to the back room where my uncle attempted to date them – which he more often than not couldn't – and provide a location if there was one and he could remember it. Then together they dreamed up titles and my dad gave each piece a number, recording all this by hand in a WHSmith ledger book.

It was a long, slow, somewhat chaotic process, hampered by a number of factors: failing memories; short, fraternal tempers; the physical obstacle course that my uncle's house had become. But slowly, over the course of a number of visits across several weeks, my dad worked his way through the rows of paintings. And then my uncle told him to go upstairs.

My dad climbed the stairs for the first time in a long time, and pushed open the door to what had been his mother's bedroom; a room he hadn't been in since her death ten years earlier. To his astonishment, he discovered it was full of as many paintings as he'd found downstairs. Then he opened the door to the spare bedroom to be greeted by the very same scene. Their work, he realised, had only just begun.

By any conventional measure, my uncle, Eric Tucker, achieved nothing in life. He never got anywhere near anything you could describe as a career. Leaving school at fourteen, he'd been apprenticed as a signwriter, but never found or took up work as one. Following national service – a compulsory stint in the army from which he briefly went AWOL – he had a string of temporary labouring jobs, eventually winding up in the delivery yard of a local construction company where he loaded and unloaded lorries. As he reached middle age, arthritis took hold and he became unable to work. What little money he had was mostly handed over to the bookmaker's. He never married, never had a partner, never had any children, never even left home; following a brief stint labouring in South Wales in his twenties, he returned to the modest council house he shared with his mother and stepfather and never left. His stepfather died in the mid-1990s, his mother in 2008, after which he lived alone in the house.

And in that house, we discovered, were more than five hundred paintings. Not just stacked up in rooms but on top of and behind wardrobes, in a stairwell cupboard and the garden shed, even stuffed into empty compost bags in the remnants of an old air raid shelter. And many hundreds of pencil drawings. Drawers were stuffed full of them, bulging sketch pads were wedged in corners and under his bed.

They were images he'd created of the world he knew, in which he was deeply immersed: working-class life in the industrial north. A world now lost. There were street scenes: intimate vignettes of life in the backstreets and alleyways, peppered with half-spectral characters playing games, walking dogs, going about their business or simply kicking their heels – smoking a cigarette and staring at the pavement under a blanket of grey. There were paintings of pub and club life: bustling, smoky interiors, vivid scenes of drinkers and revellers. There were portraits of pigeon fanciers, surreal montages of clowns and carnival workers, pictures of down-and-outs, cabaret turns, Travellers, broad-shouldered housewives in headscarves, and slightly haunting, hobbled children. He'd quietly produced this work over the course of nearly sixty years, unguided by any tutelage save for the work he saw and admired in books and galleries, and uninfluenced by involvement in even the most modest of art scenes. Among his peers, he had no one with whom he discussed the subject; most people he knew were not even aware that he painted. Much of the work was accomplished. Many of the paintings were of quite astonishing quality. And the overwhelming majority had been seen by nobody but him.

CHAPTER 2

WOULD THE MAN FROM THE NEW YORK TIMES *LIKE SOME SANDWICHES?*

In 2015, the Royal Society of Arts compiled its first 'Heritage Index' – a list ranking towns, cities and areas of the UK by quantity of cultural assets relative to geographic size. Bottom of the list, at number 325, was Warrington, my uncle's hometown, and the place I was born and raised. It was official: we were, according to the press, 'Britain's Worst Town for Culture'. In something of a pile-on, *The Times*, the *Mail*, the *Independent*, and the *Guardian* all ran some version of that headline, though the *Guardian* at least charitably added a question mark.

Warrington was found to have no listed parks, no areas of natural beauty, and – and this one really stings – no listed pubs. We didn't even have a battlefield. Of all the countless fights that have taken place in the town, none were historically notable. Jonathan Schifferes, associate director of the RSA, did note that Warrington scored well in a category called 'culture and memories', relating to 'intangible' heritage. That was perhaps meant to soften the blow, but it rather feels like it drives it home. The point is this: if there's a more unlikely place for the story of an artist to begin – and a less favourable place for someone with artistic inclinations to find themselves – then the Royal Society of Arts has yet to find it. Welcome to Warrington.

A predominantly working-class town in north-west England, Warrington is a place people mostly pass through without stopping, on the road between Liverpool and Manchester, on the train from London to Glasgow. A former industrial town, it is now arguably best known for its IKEA – the first in Britain, the town council's website boasts – and as the perplexing target of an IRA bombing in 1993 that killed two children and injured fifty-four other people.

It is part of a network of northern towns, also including Widnes, Wigan and St Helens, where rugby league and not football is the official sport. In that way, it can feel a little cut off from the mainstream. New trends take a while to permeate the town, old traditions survive there longer. Warrington still holds an annual 'walking day', an event dating back to the 1830s which sees church groups and brass bands march through the town centre while spectators line the streets. Much of what my uncle painted of the town is still discernible if you search for it – the long streets of red-brick terraced houses and their cobbled back alleys, the shells of old factories and workshops. And on a recent visit I was struck by the incongruous sight of a circus big top in the car park of a modern retail estate.

In my early twenties, I left the area. I moved to London to go to film school, stayed there and became a scriptwriter. It seemed as though to do anything interesting or exciting you had to leave. Growing up in Warrington, it could feel like a place where not much happens. And on those seldom occasions the town bothers the national consciousness, it's rarely for positive reasons. Lack of cultural assets might be the least of it. Shortly after the Heritage Index, Warrington was in the news again when police foiled a terror plot to kill an MP by a far-right group who secretly met in a pub in the town. One of our many unlisted pubs. And again when Viola Beach, a promising young indie band from the town, were tragically killed in a car accident while on tour. Kris Leonard, the band's singer, once aptly described our hometown as 'very grey and industrial', a place where there is 'nothing to do other than drink cider and smoke rollies in the park'. That's an unlisted park, don't forget.

A specific memory from my childhood might best sum up what it is to come from a place like Warrington – the mindset it yields. My family and I had gathered excitedly around the television because we'd heard that, tonight, Warrington was going to be mentioned on *Coronation Street*. It was big news – as if someone we knew personally were appearing on the iconic soap. We watched every episode together, but we watched this one with an unprecedented anticipation that left us barely able to follow the storyline. God forbid we should miss the moment. And then finally it came. 'You've got a face like a wet Wednesday in Warrington,' zinged Curly Watts. We were delighted. Thoroughly satisfied and then some. The fact that our hometown had been used as the butt of an alliterative insult hardly registered. Like an audience member picked on by a stand-up comedian, we were simply pleased to have been noticed. You get the picture:

not much happens in Warrington. So when it does, like a stone thrown into still water, the ripples are felt.

Some sixteen months after my uncle died, I travelled up from London to my old hometown. It was a chilly November morning and I was standing outside Warrington Bank Quay station, in the shadow of the Unilever washing powder factory, the last, imposing vestige of the town's soap manufacturing history – a teal-blue edifice that seems to be rusting before your eyes. Something incredibly exciting was about to happen, something I couldn't have even imagined sixteen months earlier: I was about to meet a journalist from the *New York Times*. He was going to write a story about my uncle. My uncle who spent his working life lifting heavy building materials and unloading lorries. I venture such a man doesn't often grace the culture pages of the *New York Times*.

I dearly hoped that Eric's work might find some posthumous validation. And by this point, there had already been some newspaper articles about his unearthed hoard of paintings. A couple of the tabloids had dubbed him 'The Secret Lowry'. But it was difficult to see how this might lead to him finding a place in the art world. My knowledge of the art establishment was thin but I was fairly sure it didn't read the *Daily Express*. But a piece in the *New York Times* felt like a game changer – a chance for his work to come to the attention of, as I saw it, the right sort of people.

With nervous anticipation, I stood watching the station's main doors, waiting for the journalist, Alex, to step out. In fact, he approached spy-like from behind me, having caught an earlier train from London to immerse himself in Warrington-ness before our meeting. He'd had a walk around and eaten a pie, he said. I suddenly had the faint sense of being visited by an anthropologist. And with his floppy hair, brogues and satchel, Alex certainly stood in contrast to our surroundings and the other people milling around the station drop-off area in tracksuits and polyester shirts. He looked, if I'm honest, a little bit like me.

Eager to supply Alex with everything he needed, I'd arranged a day of interviews for him – with my dad; with Buller Crompton, my uncle's friend of old; and with his neighbours, Kevin the postman and Kevin's wife Debbie. I'd told as few people as possible about the visiting journalist. And I'd asked those I had told to keep it to themselves. I can't say exactly why I did that. It wasn't based on any great logic, just a feeling. A feeling that perhaps you're inclined to if you're from a place like Warrington. That you'd better hedge your bets against such an opportunity going, in some unknowable way, horribly wrong.

We met my dad at the local museum. Alex took a look at some of Eric's paintings. Much better, he said, than he'd expected. Then the three of us headed to Shelly's, a nearby café. We found a table in a corner and Alex set about interviewing my dad as I headed for the counter to order teas.

Shelly's café is a cosy, homely space named after its larger-than-life proprietor, a lady so disarmingly chatty that later, before we left, she breezily told me about her son's ability to disassemble and reassemble a rifle without it, in that moment, seeming odd. Shelly took my order and, as I tapped the card machine to pay, she leaned across the counter and whispered to me, 'Would the man from the *New York Times* like some sandwiches for his journey home?' I was momentarily speechless. Shelly, it appeared, was in on the secret.

I returned to the table with our teas. Not long after I'd taken a seat, a man who'd been sitting alone across the room cautiously approached us and politely interrupted. He had recognised my dad, he said, from a picture in the local free newspaper, the boldly named *Warrington Worldwide*. He then announced – and with hindsight, he perhaps should've opened with this – that he was the founder and editor of *Warrington Worldwide*. 'And you must be,' he said without missing a beat, thrusting a hand towards Alex, 'the man from the *New York Times*.' At which point Shelly arrived at the table with two complimentary fondant fancies stuffed into a Tupperware box – for Alex to enjoy on the Pendolino home. I realised that my efforts to keep it on the down-low had been futile. The whole of Warrington seemed to know that the *New York Times* had come to town. We were buffeting Alex with guileless attempts at charm, hoping he could sprinkle a little magic dust, gushing with gratitude for his very presence and the rare prospect of a little prestige.

We left my dad, and I drove Alex to King George Crescent, the sleepy loop of pre-war council houses where my uncle had lived since the 1950s. We took a tour of what had been his house, courtesy of its new owners

– a young couple in the midst of renovating the place, who welcomed us in with a friendliness that, if you've lived in London for more than ten years, is almost traumatising. The idea was to give Alex some sense of the place where my uncle had produced all his artwork; the modest front room that had been his hermetic workshop. But so extensive were the renovations, including the removal of walls, that we found ourselves effectively just admiring some very competent DIY.

Next, we wandered across the street for a chat with Kevin and Debbie, who were high on my uncle's list of approved neighbours. Debbie, a professional carer, was one of the few people my uncle, in his final years, would allow in the house to help him. She explained how this had led her to discover, after many years of knowing him, that he was a painter. Kevin, meanwhile, with commendable honesty, declared all art to be beyond him. Asked what, if anything, he knew of my uncle's artistic activities, he recalled a distant memory of a painted horse appearing in the window of a local bookmaker's, long since closed. He had the idea – he'd heard on the grapevine – that the artist was Eric, the man who lived across the street with his parents. This story was news to me but my mum later confirmed it. The council had ordered the painting to be removed, she recalled, because passing cars were slowing to admire it.

We then went to see my uncle's friend, Buller Crompton, spending a while driving around in the drizzle as I tried to find Buller's bungalow among an indistinct maze of sheltered accommodation. When I finally found it, Buller greeted us at the door, propped up behind a Zimmer frame. Buller is my uncle's oldest surviving friend, the two having met when they joined the same boxing club as teenagers. Spending time with him is a little like hanging out with my uncle's ghost. He has the same solid, boxer's build. He speaks with the same old south Lancashire accent and vernacular, referring to me – affectionately, I promise – as 'cock'. He hasn't cultivated – or else succumbed to – the same dishevelled mien as my uncle, but I did notice he used a J-Cloth as a handkerchief.

We shuffled behind Buller into his living room, where we found a three-piece suite in an unusual arrangement. A two-seater sofa had its back to the wall on our left as we entered the room. But it was largely inaccessible due to a wooden chair plonked directly in front of it; the only chair, Buller explained, that he was able to sit in. That left two large armchairs, which Alex and I took, but these were positioned with their backs to the sofa, like cinema seating. It meant that the entire conservation was conducted with Alex and I leaning back over our shoulders to face Buller, sitting in his wooden chair behind and between us. It was as if the old man had decided that his interview with the *New York Times* would be staged in the manner of a pretend car.

Alex pressed on, admirably undeterred by the unusual arrangement. But though the interview survived the challenge of unorthodox seating, it struggled to bridge a cultural divide. I tried to act as a sort of conduit, helping to elucidate for Alex any of Buller's answers that assumed intimate knowledge of Warrington or the world of amateur boxing. And after some of Alex's questions, Buller would turn to me with a look of unabashed bewilderment, appealing to me for a translation or maybe just an ally.

'Do you think Eric painted because he had to?' Alex asked Buller softly, hopeful perhaps that the old boxer might muse on the mystifying impulses behind artistic creation.

'No!' cried Buller, throwing me one of his glances, 'He did it because he wanted to!'

I had the feeling that perhaps we weren't giving Alex what he was looking for. That everything after the pie may have failed to meet expectations.

Early the following week, Alex called to tell me that, unfortunately, the paper wouldn't be running the story. I felt my heart sink into my stomach. I was disappointed, to put it mildly. I'd convinced myself this was my uncle's one real shot at an entrée to the art world. I felt I'd let the old man down. And thinking back to the encounters in Shelly's café, I also felt slightly responsible for raising what seemed like the whole town's hopes. Having grown up there, I know how much sustenance a small town can draw from the slightest morsel of glamour.

Alex said his editor had pulled the article feeling that it wasn't the story he'd expected. He was expecting, I think, a Henry Darger figure. Darger was the quintessential 'outsider artist', a poor hospital janitor from Chicago whose cache of fantastical writing and artwork was discovered at the end of his life. Or Vivian Maier, the American street photographer who worked as a nanny, her photographs only coming to public attention after her death. Eric's story had something in common with these. And to be fair, the tabloid articles that had caught Alex's attention had called him 'The Secret Lowry'. In a tabloidy nutshell, it wasn't exactly wrong. But it wasn't exactly right either – the story was more complicated. My uncle had, for the most part, been highly unforthcoming about his work. But he had also made some attempts over the years, albeit rather few and far between, to show and sell his work. Given this, Alex said his editor had concluded that my uncle was therefore 'just a guy who failed'.

It stung to hear. Specifically the word 'just'. More specifically because I doubted my uncle had been given the chance to fail, much less to succeed. On behalf of him, I was feeling something previously blissfully unknown to me: indignation at someone with little understanding of your life experience telling you how you've had it.

Ultimately, I felt I couldn't complain. The man was just doing his job. Editors gonna edit. But in other, more visceral ways, I felt: how many other unskilled labourers, this week, have been discovered to have quietly produced a sizeable hoard of surprisingly accomplished artwork?! The editor's assessment seemed to say that an artist like my uncle had to be indubitably mysterious and strange or their story wasn't worth telling – which to me was evidence itself of why it needed to be told. Moreover, the inconsistencies in Eric's attitude, and the fact his story was difficult to neatly summarise, were for me part of what made it intriguing.

However, precisely none of these arguments, even if I'd had the wherewithal to make them, was going to help me on the phone with Alex. I had the horrible feeling of a natural order reasserting itself. It was the same feeling that had caused me to try to keep his visit quiet in the first place: that same wariness of the spectre of success. My uncle knew this feeling. Born on a Friday the 13th, he sometimes joked that his luck hadn't changed since. Was this the curse's latest manifestation? As if to confirm that it might be, Alex mentioned something else before our call ended.

His trip to Warrington hadn't been entirely wasted, he told me. He'd been working on an article about the Benin Bronzes – African cultural artefacts that were looted by colonialist British forces in the nineteenth century. Alex thought he might have spotted one in a display case at Warrington Museum. He was going to investigate further. Fantastic, I thought. Far from furnishing the town with a rare cultural news story in a prestigious paper, it seemed I might have unwittingly arranged for its cash-strapped museum – one of our few 'tangible' cultural assets – to be cancelled.

Looking through my uncle's work shortly after his death, I had wondered where he might fit into the art world. It had occurred to me that perhaps he was an 'outsider artist'. As a former art student, I was familiar with outsider art, but it's a weird thought to have about someone you've actually known. The term – an English equivalent to the earlier French expression *art brut* – was coined by critic Roger Cardinal in the early 1970s and has been extremely successful in promoting work by self-taught, usually naive artists from outside the mainstream art world; in presenting these artists to the mainstream art world, you could say, in a way that arguably accentuates their mysterious otherness.

In some ways, the label seemed to fit my uncle very well. In others, it didn't. His was almost the archetypal outsider artist story – but it also wasn't exactly. By the same measure, his work was tricky to place – at once both naive and sophisticated. I mentioned these thoughts to my dad. 'Well, he's not some curio!' my dad replied. A key factor in the mythologising of outsider artists may be that they don't have too many close relatives. Understandably, I think my dad felt that his brother's work deserved to be considered not just curious and fascinating, but meaningful and good – and in its own context. He was right – but was that possible for a man who unloaded lorries? The experience with the *New York Times* seemed to suggest we faced a struggle.

We were left with no clear sense of a path to pursue, no idea of how we might bring all this work, utterly unknown to the world, to anyone's attention. The task was completely overwhelming. But I also felt an inkling, buried underneath the doubt and uncertainty, that my uncle's luck was about to change.

My uncle, as a character, was slippery to define. He was a bundle of contradictions. So perhaps it's not surprising that his story is too. He had always been a conundrum, but the unearthing of all his paintings greatly amplified the fact. It raised questions – or made those I already had feel much more compelling. Why had he been so possessive and paranoid about his work? Why did he make so few attempts to promote it – and yet make any at all? Had he wanted his paintings to be seen, or was he indifferent, or even – as he had sometimes seemed – opposed to it? And what had driven him to sustain such a committed practice, over decades, with seemingly little thought – or hope – of recognition? It was like a chef quietly honing their craft, making meals to be indefinitely frozen. What was it all for?

When people asked me why he was so unforthcoming about his art, I couldn't give them a good answer. The best I could offer, with a shrug, was: 'It's just the way he was.' And if he'd left behind a handful of pictures, that might have sufficed. But in the face of an avalanche, it didn't. *Why* was it the way he was?

In the days following Alex's phone call, I confess that I sent a somewhat undignified email to his editor, looking to plead my case, in hopes that he might reconsider. Chances seemed slim but, as my uncle's advocate – and God knows he needed one – I couldn't live with myself if I hadn't at least given it a shot. Though on reflection, perhaps I was doing this more for me than him. This was the validation *I* wanted for my uncle and his work – the audience *I* wanted him to reach. What he might have wanted was much harder to say.

The editor sent back a short reply to my email, briefly restating the facts – that he'd sent a reporter 'up to Liverpool' but decided not to do anything. Liverpool – great city though it is – was the final straw. A new resolve was roused in me. As a scriptwriter, I was sure I knew a good story. So why was I trying to persuade someone else to write this one? Was I too close to this story to tell it? Maybe. But I was beginning to think you could also be too far.

This book is the story of my uncle from the point I knew him, and the remarkable events that began the day he tentatively raised the prospect of an exhibition, aged eighty-four. It's also an investigation into how he became the man he was, an attempt to understand what formed such an apparently very ordinary but in fact rather extraordinary, equivocal, exasperating character. And perhaps in doing so, to reveal something about the nature of creativity, the power of art and who it belongs to. Though I confess my motives aren't entirely noble.

I'm reminded of a scene in the Wes Anderson film *The Life Aquatic with Steve Zissou*. The titular oceanographer announces to an audience his intention to hunt down and kill the shark who ate his right-hand man. An audience member politely asks him what the scientific purpose of such a mission would be. Zissou thinks for a moment and then, with a shrug, he says, 'Revenge.'

CHAPTER 3

UNCLE ERIC

An uncle is a slightly nebulous figure in your life. It's an ill-defined role. They're not like your parents, with the authority. And they're not like your grandparents, with the doting. They might be a frequent presence in your life, or someone you only see at Christmas; close and well known to you, or a distant, rather mysterious character. And in some cases, both.

As a child, my mum once, maybe twice, casually informed me that if she and my dad were to die – in a car accident, for example – I would go to live with my uncle. Not my uncle Eric but her older brother, Terry. The thought filled me with quiet horror. Partly because it seemed there was enough chance of my parents dying in a car accident that a contingency plan was required. Partly as I tried to imagine my orphaned life with another family.

Don't misunderstand me, I was fond of my uncle Terry. He held a family party every Christmas. It marked the start of the festive season with well-organised games and an impressive buffet. Also, he was an early adopter of technology, owning both a Casio keyboard and a VHS camcorder before anyone else I knew. He didn't really seem to know how to work either. But, crucially, both were passed on to me. And gratefully accepted – though I must admit, with a sense that he could've given them up a little sooner. Nevertheless, it was still unnerving to

UNCLE ERIC

imagine myself entirely under his guardianship. And on reflection, it's telling that the candidate for this backup plan was not the uncle I saw most often, who was undoubtedly my favourite: Eric.

My earliest memories of my uncle Eric are of time spent at his house – my grandparents' house – as a preschooler. Of pestering him to spoon-feed me the stew my nanna had cooked, even though I could now feed myself. Or sending balloons flying along pieces of string stretched through the house, trying for more improbable flights on longer lengths of string.

Fourteen King George Crescent, where he lived with my grandparents, was a featureless red-brick council house on the end of a short terrace; an almost perfectly square box with poky, unsymmetrically placed windows, set back from the street by a short concrete path and a garden compact enough to be overshadowed by wheelie bins. It had three rooms downstairs including the L-shaped kitchen. The nucleus of the house, however, from which my grandparents rarely moved, was the back room. Each had their own armchair in there, either side of the boxy gas fireplace. My nanna was by the telephone, my grandad was next to a chest of drawers – within easy reach of a pack of cards and a large nebuliser he used to treat his asthma.

My parents both worked so, as a child, I spent a lot of time at both sets of grandparents' houses. My favourite was Nanna and Grandad Urey's house – my dad's and Eric's mother and stepfather. And the great treat of going there was that I got to spend time with Eric.

He would school me in drawing, how to fill in a football coupon, why none of today's fighters would last two rounds against Harry Grebb, what I could expect from a Ken Dodd live show. Long sermons on the latter. Often recounting for me great swathes of Doddy's act and the masterful effect it had on his audience, with my grandmother chipping in from her armchair to agree. All delivered as if preparing me – getting me suitably hyped up – for the day when I myself would inevitably go to a live performance by the great man. Which I regret now that I never did. Though I almost didn't need to.

Spending time with my uncle, the next laugh was never far away. Comedy was a great love of his and he had a strong streak of club comic running through him. Not to mention encyclopaedic recall of his favourite comedians' jokes to supplement his own material – the two often being difficult to tell apart. He also had an intuitive eye for the absurd. I remember he once presented me with a picture he'd torn from the *Sunday Times Magazine* – a macro-focus photograph of an unborn baby that, he pointed out, bore an uncanny resemblance to Del Boy Trotter. The undeniable accuracy of this left me helpless and the image was duly saved among the magazines under the TV, regularly resurfacing on request for an instant hit of amusement.

Most days I spent at the house followed the same pattern. We ate lunch at an oddly early hour, around 11 a.m. I often lobbied for even greater indulgence of this eccentricity, sometimes pushing it as early as ten. My nanna generally made the same meal for me every time: liver and onion stew with two slices of buttered white bread. It became such a fixture that, if she did try to vary the offering, I was livid. After our early lunch, Eric would take my nanna and me on a 'run out' in his car. We usually went to a nearby garden centre. They would have a cup of tea in the café, while I strained to look at 'Magic Eye' pictures – novelty optical illusions that were, for some reason, sold in garden centres at the time – and my uncle would stuff his pockets full of complimentary sachets of sugar as if rationing were still in force.

My grandad never joined us on these little jaunts. He always stayed behind at the house. That didn't occur to me as odd at the time but, as I got a little older, I grew more conscious of it. I noticed that there was something strange about Eric's and my grandad's relationship. I never witnessed any cross words between them but, in fact, I never saw them exchange many words at all. Eric very occasionally offered his stepfather a cup of tea when making a round – that's about as much as I remember them interacting. And even these brief exchanges seemed oddly terse. Most of the time, the two men barely acknowledged one another – a feat all the more remarkable for the fact that the house was so small and they all largely lived in the one back room of it.

It wasn't just at his house that I regularly saw my uncle. Then in his fifties, he had not long since stopped working on grounds of ill health: chronic arthritis preventing him from continuing as a labourer. Hence why he was at home every day when I was there – bar the odd occasion when I would arrive to find he was out, and feel distinctly short-changed. But it also meant that he was quite often at our house, helping my parents by babysitting or carrying out odd jobs. Most times this help was sought, but sometimes he imposed it. I remember each summer he would remove the wasps' nest from the large tree at the end of our garden. He had learned the price my dad had paid the council to do it and simply refused to allow his brother to submit to this robbery again. The operation amazed me. It was one he seemed to carry out with little more than a pair of gardening gloves and a plastic carrier bag. I would watch from a safe distance as he extracted the nest, boiling with wasps. Then he'd tie it up in the carrier bag and sling it in the back seat of his car to be driven to the tip. Years later I thought to ask him, didn't he get stung on the journey? 'Yeah,' he answered, looking at me like the question was a daft one. For a man without a family of his own, he had an extraordinary sense of familial duty. Perhaps he liked to have a reason to be in our lives but it seemed to go deeper than that: something had instilled in him an urgent sense that family must stick together.

Despite his arthritis, Eric still looked pretty robust at this time. He was still recognisably a man who, in his youth, had been a boxer. He was dishevelled but not yet dilapidated. To me this was his classic look – the way he is fixed in my mind – and it was a somewhat jarring mix. There was something of the Alan Bennett character about him, with his stretched-out BHS jumper, his straggly, self-cut hair, and the fact he was so often in tandem with his mother. But he was also strong, his rolled-up shirt-sleeves revealed muscular forearms, tanned like a farm labourer's, with chunky copper bracelets on each wrist which were meant to alleviate his arthritis.

He picked me up from primary school every day, bringing my nanna along for the ride, and there was a time when both his jacket and a smashed rear passenger window of his car were held together with yellowing Sellotape. He referred to the latter as 'the stained-glass window'. You might think I'd be embarrassed by this but, actually, nothing could be further from the truth. I thought it was brilliant. I wholeheartedly believed he had the right take on life.

By contrast, I considered my uncle Terry to have all the wrong priorities. He was the total inverse of Eric – always smartly dressed, a member of the Rotary Club, the kind of man to wear a tie with a crest on it. When we went out for a family meal, to a pub-restaurant, Terry would produce a small black notebook to jot down everyone's drink order before going to the bar. My mum was bowled over by this. The first time it happened she spoke at length on the car journey home about what an excellent idea it was – a clear improvement on my dad trying to hold everyone's order in his head, dashing back from the bar a couple of times to check, and inevitably still getting one or two wrong. But for me, it was the epitome of where my uncle Terry was going wrong in life. In fact, he was a successful architect with a large house in a posh suburb of Manchester. He had achieved this from beginnings almost as humble and unforgiving as my uncle Eric. It was, I came to appreciate much later, an amazing achievement. But this was lost on me as a child – or at least meant nothing – because he brought stationery to the pub.

My uncle Eric's approach to life was very different. His was a philosophy seemingly at odds with the world at large, though despite this (or maybe because of it) he had astonishing conviction in it. As far as he was concerned, it was among the very lowest echelons of society that the richest life was to be found. That's where you wanted to be. For him, it was an almost perfectly inverse ratio: the lower you stooped, the better it got. This applied to everything. My dad, for example, might invite him to a nice restaurant, for his birthday perhaps, telling him how good the food was. 'Tony, Tony, Tony,' my uncle would say, shaking his head, 'life's passin' yer by.' Then he'd recall what he felt to be one of the truly great dining experiences of his life, the commendations invariably coming down to three things: the price – cheap; the portion sizes – vast; the clientele – impoverished. 'Real rough-and-ready people,' he'd say, by way of recommendation.

Among the family, he didn't have many allies in his unconventional outlook. In fact, he had precisely none. Except for one: me. I was entirely sold on this worldview – my principal reasons being, to my mind, manifestly evident in the man himself. But events also frequently proved it to me further. To give just one example: he and my dad took me and a friend for a walk in the countryside one day. We got lost – which, mapless and trespassing freely, seemed to be half the aim – and had to take shelter, in beating rain, under the covered gateway of a church. We were stranded – until a passing truck driver recognised my uncle and gave us a lift. I was impossibly impressed. He seemed to know the world.

In truth, my uncle was so present in my life at this time that he was almost a third parent, providing an alternate set of values to the liberal, middle-class upbringing my mum was working hard to cultivate. I remember one day piously recounting that week's Quaker

Sunday School lesson to him: turn the other cheek. Do not meet violence with violence. He physically stopped me in my tracks, grasped my shoulders and looked me square in the face. 'Joe,' he said, 'if someone hits you, you *always* hit them back.' In seconds, forty-five minutes of gently instilled Christian doctrine was overturned.

My uncle even came on holiday with us every year to Pembrokeshire. We stayed in a bunkhouse where, to my scandalised delight, he would sometimes draw on the MDF underside of the bunk bed above. In the evenings, when my parents were deep in conversation, he and I would hang out in the kitchen. He'd make me cheese on toast, slicing the cheddar thrillingly thick like a hunk of hewn stone. He felt to me almost like a member of our immediate family, which might make it seem all the more incredible that we were unaware of the scale of his artistic output until the very end of his life. But there were aspects of the situation – and more pertinently his character – that made this entirely feasible.

Though we saw him often, how he led his own life in between times was something of a mystery to us. Even when we were on holiday together in Pembrokeshire, he would often slip off by himself – maintain a certain distance. We would stumble across him on the coastal path. Or, when dinner was ready, I'd be dispatched to fetch him from the roughest pub in town – where, he had discovered, they would illegally take a bet. He had sought familiar surroundings, found the underlying Eric-ness in even a picture postcard holiday spot, while we were visiting Welsh craft centres and trying to surf.

He was almost one of us – but he was ultimately

separate. We weren't exactly his people. Also, there was just something interminably solitary about him. His great sociability, and love of socialising, easily led you to overlook it. But the eventual discovery of all his artwork underlined the fact, evidence as it was of great swathes of time spent alone. He was loved by the family, but there was no family unit into which he easily fit. On holiday with us, he was the add-on. In his home too, he was an awkward addition.

As a child, it never struck me as odd that my uncle lived with his parents. That was just how it was. More to the point, so did I. I wonder now if part of what made me feel such camaraderie with him was that there was something a little childlike about him, at least in this aspect of his life. Though there was nothing about him to suggest he couldn't live on his own. He was more than capable of looking after himself and, in fact, very independent; an irrepressibly free spirit. He could've afforded his own place, just about. But the fact is that if he could have left home then he surely would have done. Something was keeping him there.

As much as I felt an affinity with my uncle, there was also much that made him seem like someone from another world or time – somehow even more so than my grandparents. He used words and slang and sang songs I'd never heard anywhere else. His bedroom looked absolutely archaic. A Victorian chamber pot peeked out from under a single bed covered in a rough, grey blanket better suited to military barracks or a prison cell. On his wall hung a framed music examination certificate, made out to a name I didn't recognise, and a card with a poem on it under the word 'Mizpah', both of them crumbling and dusty. The room contained two chests of drawers and two wardrobes – one more of each than it could comfortably accommodate. Pinned to the wardrobes were fading posters, like a teenager's bedroom – though not of pop stars or pin-ups, but art exhibitions.

There was another room in the house that was entirely Eric's domain, one we rarely went in: his painting room. It was in this modest space, hidden behind a lace curtain and under a single bulb, that my uncle produced all of his paintings. For a brief period in the distant past, it had been my grandparents' front parlour, a room traditionally 'kept for best' – Sundays and special occasions. The evidence of that was still just about discernible. There were a couple of sideboards at the edges of the room – one, glass-fronted, was still full of 1950s ornaments. Undecorated since that time, the room had textured wallpaper, dark brown floorboards and a threadbare rug. In the centre stood my uncle's easel, a wooden chair and a small table scattered with brushes and half-spent tubes of oil paint. Fanning out from there, and building to something of a crescendo at the edges, was a mess of books, newspapers, sketch pads, pieces of torn-edged paper and other items too miscellaneous to list. Among this, paintings were stacked up in rows on the floor. Or were they unpainted boards? It was difficult to tell as one covered the next.

The frosted glass door to the room wasn't generally shut but was always pulled to – a result, perhaps, of the frequency with which my uncle slipped in and out. Though in all the long hours and days I spent at the house, I don't remember seeing him paint even once. I think now that he surely must have done, at times when I was absorbed in watching television or drawing, and so quietly that I didn't notice.

As an uninhibited young child, I would occasionally swan in there, to pinch a pencil or some paper, or just mooch around the jumble of things so old and obscure they seemed to me otherworldly. Like a vortex that sucked in stuff, I might happen on something of my own – a *Beano* annual I'd forgotten about among the dusty books and magazines.

When I was a little older, I'd go with my dad to visit the house on Sunday evenings. Eric always answered the door, then shouted back to my nanna that it was carol singers or the coal men. On our way to the back room, my dad sometimes made it his business to go into his brother's painting room and have a look at what was on the easel. He'd offer a few words of encouragement or try to open a conversation. But Eric would hover in the doorway saying very little – or even nothing – in response. Gone was the man joking that carol singers had turned up in October.

Here was one of my uncle's many contradictions: he was a gregarious raconteur, unafraid to express firm opinions, but when it came to this matter he was silent. He never spoke about his work. I never heard him tell anyone he was a painter. He didn't appear to exactly mind us coming into his painting room like this, but he certainly didn't invite it. He never brought a finished painting out of the room to show us. In fact, in all the time I knew him, he never drew my attention to a single one of his pictures – though when I was in my twenties, he did gift a couple to me without comment.

For most visitors to the house, with the door to the front room pulled to, there was practically no evidence of a painter in the family. I remember only one of Eric's paintings being on display, halfway up the stairs at the turn in the staircase. It was a small portrait of a young African boy – a relatively early effort, possibly copied from *National Geographic*, realistic and skilfully executed but somewhat lost among the other kitschy wall decorations. I can imagine my grandmother feeling it was justifiably artistic, at least much more so than the images he would later produce. For the most part, Eric's work didn't leave the workshop, even in his own house. It would appear he finished a painting, added it to a stack of others, and moved on to the next. And repeat – for sixty years. Though there was a notable exception around this time.

In 1995 my uncle, then sixty-three, entered a painting into an open-call art exhibition at the local museum and art gallery. It was the first and only time I'd known him to publicly share his work. I seem to recall my dad had seen an article about the exhibition in the local newspaper which he shared with his brother, gently encouraging him to enter. I dimly remember him placing it on the sideboard one Sunday when we visited, with a 'thought you might be interested in this, Eric'. And Eric muttering vague appreciation, but not picking up or looking at the paper in the time we were there. (I've half a memory that it was in exactly the same spot when we returned the following Sunday.) You had to tread carefully in such endeavours with my uncle. By this time, it was received wisdom in the family that you couldn't help him – with anything really, but especially not his painting. It was more trouble than it was worth. He wouldn't welcome the intervention. But on this occasion, at least, the encouragement appeared to work. The next thing we knew, a painting he had quietly submitted had been accepted into the show. And following this, it was purchased for the museum's collection. He had effectively 'won' the exhibition. Though he didn't tell us that part, as I recall. My mum spotted it when we attended the show's opening, at which Eric was absent.

Any effect this had on him was difficult to discern. There were no celebrations. I don't recall even a gratified smile. And it didn't obviously appear to galvanise him to further promote his work in other ways. If anything, he grew more possessive of his paintings from here on, as if his brief taste of success had confirmed for him that he'd better be extra vigilant.

Shortly before the open-call exhibition, there was a significant event in my young life, one which is pertinent to this stage in my relationship with my uncle: my pet rabbit, Rollo, died. I had wanted a dog, but this wasn't allowed on grounds of my brother's allergies, so Rollo was the compensatory offering. And he did fall short of a dog, it must be said. It was hard to really bond with Rollo – he was almost constantly frightened and he lived outside. And on occasions when we let him run free in the garden, it quickly became clear he felt little attachment to us. My dad would spend a good hour trying to extract him from under shrubbery while I blocked off the garden's exits. But still, I loved Rollo, and I was anxious to ensure he was properly laid to rest.

We lived in a rented house at the time, which we were about to leave, so my mum suggested burying him at my grandparents' house. The thought horrified me. The backyard at King George Crescent was small and a little scruffy. It was overlooked by neighbours, one of whom Eric was convinced had stolen a wheel from his car. How that threatened a dead rabbit, I'm not sure, but it just altogether didn't seem befitting of a place of rest. Then I hit on the perfect solution: the spacious gardens of my uncle Terry's house in the posh suburb of Manchester. A place I hardly visited more than once a year but much more suitable, I thought, for the interment of a beloved pet.

Something had changed in me. The world had begun to win me around to its way of thinking and away from my uncle Eric's. Not long after this, my family moved out of Warrington to a house in the nearby countryside, and I went to high school. I no longer needed to be picked up from school by my uncle. Or go to my grandparents' house afterwards. And in many ways, my uncle and I would never again be so close as we had been.

Twenty-six years later, sorting through the piles of drawings we had found in his house, I was surprised to discover one of me. Based on my first-year high school photograph, and deftly executed – I hadn't realised how good a draughtsman he was until after his death – it showed me just as I was at this time. Back when I was still, just about, my uncle's guy.

Our family lore that Eric couldn't be helped – that you shouldn't get involved with his artistic endeavours – was well established by the time I arrived. It seemed to mainly rest on an incident, more than a decade before the open-call exhibition, in which my dad had tried to help his brother sell some work through a gallery in Manchester. And what an unmitigated disaster this had been, with my dad swearing off trying anything like it again. The principal exponent of this story, as I recall, was my mum – though certainly nobody disagreed. And it seemed to me to fit the profile. But what exactly had happened in this incident before my time? How had it gone wrong? And could it provide any insight into my uncle's apparent reticence around sharing his art?

CHAPTER 4

YOU'VE GOTTA WATCH THESE BUGGERS

The story of my dad's ill-fated attempt to help his brother is the story of the one time in my uncle's life – that we know of – when he tried to establish a relationship with an art dealer; the one time he'd been known to promote his work by his own motivation. My dad was hazy on exactly when it happened. Sometime in the late 1970s or early 1980s, he thought. My uncle was then in his late forties or early fifties and still working, at the time, for a local construction company, Monk – or 'Monks's', as he referred to it. In light of his arthritis, he'd been relieved of his original duties, loading and unloading lorries at the depot, and instead sent out on site deliveries where the journey provided a longer break between the heavy lifting. Somehow, after shifts, he found the energy to paint – something he'd been doing by this time for more than twenty years. But this story really begins a decade or so earlier, when my uncle started to frequent Manchester's private art galleries: galleries offering work for sale, several of which were dotted through the streets of the city centre.

Manchester was then undergoing a difficult metamorphosis, trying to regenerate itself from its vanishing industrial past into the modern city it would become. Manufacturing jobs were disappearing and the population was decreasing. Boarded-up buildings were submerged under flyposters, others lay in piles of rubble awaiting new development. There were bustling shops and nightclubs but it was then a less sanitised Manchester, full of seedy enclaves, its underbelly more visible.

Each Saturday, Eric would take a train to the city. He'd visit one or other of its two public galleries: The Whitworth or Manchester City Art Gallery, as it was then known. It was in these two galleries that he educated himself in art. He came to know their permanent collections well. *Work*, by the Victorian painter Ford Madox Brown – a busy street scene capturing the totality of British society, with labourers at its centre – was a particular favourite, my dad told me.

After this he'd hit the pubs and clubs, often not returning home until the next day. Occasionally my dad joined him. They'd see an exhibition together and drink a few pints. Then my dad would catch the train home, he told me, leaving his brother alone in the city. What exactly he got up to, my dad wasn't sure. But likely the characters he caroused with after hours had little idea he'd spent the afternoon studying Pre-Raphaelites.

At some point, a tour of Manchester's private galleries was added to this itinerary. It began, perhaps, when one caught his eye in the side streets surrounding the city's main public gallery. He slowly graduated from peering in their windows to venturing inside – a step my dad believed would have been a huge challenge for his brother. Most people, I think, feel at least a little intimidated by such places. It's not like walking into a Tesco Metro. They're usually empty enough that you can only make a conspicuous entrance. Is the attendant behind the desk making a swift assessment of your finances? Almost certainly. For Eric, these feelings were amplified a thousandfold. He felt himself to be very far from the galleries' clients – the city's well-off professionals and businessfolk – but also, more to the point, from their artists. So what motivated him to cross the threshold? It seems like he must have been harbouring some ambition, however small and closely guarded, to see his work on their walls. But I can imagine he had to gradually warm himself up to these feelings – by familiarising himself with the galleries' work, comparing it to his own, and slowly coming to feel comfortable in his surroundings.

Over time, he became a regular visitor. And to one gallery in particular: the Tib Lane Gallery – then the city's longest-established and most respected fine art dealer. His ambition may have been highly tentative, but it seems he was lining up for the bullseye. And on one visit to this gallery, he had a fleeting encounter that seems strangely portentous on this journey.

It was a late afternoon – the quiet couple of hours when the daytime shoppers are drifting home and the night-time revellers are yet to roll in. The gallery was silent and my uncle was alone, absorbed in a painting, when he suddenly became aware of someone else in the room – some small sound or perhaps just a feeling that caused him to turn around. Standing there, looking at him, was a tall, old man in a long mac – a man he felt he recognised.

'I've never worked, you know,' the old man said matter-of-factly. And my uncle realised he was face to face with L.S. Lowry.

My uncle struggled to understand Lowry's comment. Startled, and not a little intimidated to meet one of Britain's most famous painters, my uncle replied humbly, 'Well, you've done your work, Mr Lowry.' He assumed the old man was being modest – expressing that his art was not a labour to him when my uncle knew that, even if this were true, Lowry had served a long apprenticeship to get there. But Lowry stared back blankly, apparently as confused by this response as my uncle had been by his initial remark.

'I've never worked,' he repeated bluntly.

A short while later, it occurred to my uncle that Lowry – who since his death some have speculated may have been autistic – meant exactly what he said: that he had never had to work to support himself as an artist. Which was in fact a lie, though my uncle didn't know it at the time. After an apprenticeship at an accountancy firm, Lowry spent his working life as a rent collector, a fact that only became publicly known after his death. Lowry had kept it a closely guarded secret after critics labelled him a 'Sunday painter'.

It was a term useful for dismissing artists who, like Lowry, weren't among the very few able to live off their artwork – or, as was more often the case, by other private means that allowed them to avoid a job. Snobbery abounded in the art world. The critic Edwin Mullins, in the catalogue introduction he wrote for Lowry's retrospective at the Tate, described Lowry's characters as 'undignified pea-brained homunculi'. No wonder Lowry was terrified they might discover he had a real job. It also gives further context to my uncle's trepidation at dipping his toe in this world by stepping inside the gallery.

My uncle told me the story of his encounter with Lowry himself, as always emphasising the humour and the curious insight into Lowry's character. But it seems particularly unfortunate that Lowry made his false boast – that he had 'never worked' – to my uncle, very much a working man. If my uncle was nurturing tentative ambitions to be represented by the gallery, as I think he must have been, then I wonder how this affected his sense of what right he had to them.

Years passed, it seems, before Eric eventually spoke to the gallery owner about his own work. It's a reflection, I think, of just how much he had to build up confidence. Among my uncle's paintings, though they were mostly unframed, I noticed that some of the early works had frames he'd built himself. Later ones he'd had professionally framed, and it struck me that even this had required him to muster courage and self-worth. Beyond this, approaching the gallery owner would have held a number of difficulties for him.

Firstly, where he felt out of his comfort zone, he was absolutely unwilling to adapt – completely averse to moderating his character. He strenuously avoided using the telephone and I'm sure this is why. It required a subtle etiquette that got in the way of his regular schtick. And he'd rather travel miles to deal with someone in person than dispense with the schtick. He didn't do etiquette; everyone was met with the same Eric Tucker and the aim was to swiftly dispense with any formality or decorum, usually through comedy. He needed to bring people 'down' to his level because he certainly wouldn't be travelling 'up' to theirs. But in the sedate and rarefied world of the private art gallery, formality and decorum are practically the stock-in-trade. And there's not much that makes the art world bristle more than a comedian. So, you can see the scale of his challenge.

When the moment finally came – of broaching the subject of his own work – it would need to feel as casual and nonchalant as possible. I can well imagine the multiple, unhurried stages leading up to this: gradually becoming such a regular visitor to the gallery that a bit of fleeting chat with the owner is inevitable. Nothing too strong at first. A few words about the weather, maybe a bit of back and forth about some of the work on display. Let the man know you know a thing or two. Not too much, mind, but more than he might expect based on your haircut and jacket. Pleasantly informed, not Brian Sewell. Maybe then establishing another common interest with him – if, on another occasion, the opportunity presents itself. Something less high-minded, more levelling. What's in your kit bag? The comedy of Ken Dodd, Jackie Mason, Bernard Manning. Risky. Sport then, perhaps. Or a chat about the pubs of Manchester – the pub being the common British interest that surely bridges all divides. And then finally, after all this, once you're comfortable that the man knows you're never going to buy anything, and you're comfortable that he's comfortable with that, one day casually mentioning that you do a bit of painting yourself. And perhaps only then because, with you having haunted the gallery for so many years, the owner finally asks.

Exactly how it happened, I don't know, but at some point my uncle asked the gallery owner if he would consider his work. When my dad was visiting the house one day, my uncle mentioned it. An offhand utterance, as if he generated this kind of opportunity more than never, followed by vague speculation on how he would get the paintings there (this was before he owned a car). My dad picked up the cue and offered to drive him. 'Aye, alright, Tony. If it's not out of your way.'

By this time, my dad had some history of trying to encourage his brother – with mixed results. Around a decade earlier, he had persuaded him to enter a painting into the Royal Academy's Summer Show. He drove my uncle all the way to London to deliver his submission. A couple of weeks later, my uncle received a rejection letter – which we found, after his death, filed away in a drawer in his painting room – and so my dad drove him all the way back to collect the work. They had a pie and a pint, my dad told me, as if that somewhat mitigated the day-long journey, and my uncle peered in the windows of the galleries of Cork Street, in the shadow of the Royal Academy – a whole other league from the galleries of Manchester. On other occasions, again hoping to encourage his brother and show support, my dad had asked if he could buy a painting. 'He didn't always respond,' my dad told me. 'He'd become guarded.' The difference now, though, was that Eric had generated this opportunity himself.

The following week, my dad drove his brother to

Manchester with three of his paintings. On the way, they stopped at a scrap merchant's, my dad remembered. It was a habit of my uncle's to amass bits of metal scavenged from building site clearances. He had brought a small stockpile to be weighed and priced up. An act of convenience, perhaps, but possibly also a chance to calibrate his nerves beforehand in an environment where he felt more comfortable.

My dad was ostensibly there to provide a lift and carry a picture or two, but really he was there for moral support. Unlike his older brother, he'd been to art school and had later gotten a degree from the Open University. He was an educated man and I suspect my uncle felt that could be something very useful to him that day – though it may be hard to admit that to your younger brother. However, my dad was keenly aware that this was unprecedented proactivity from his brother and must be handled delicately. Eric would need to feel in full control of the situation. So once they were in the gallery, my dad hung back. He browsed the work on display and let his brother speak to the gallery owner. Though of course, he was listening intently.

The gallery owner looked over my uncle's paintings – and my uncle. He was hesitant. He seemed unsure. There were already a number of artists around who were similar in style to Lowry, he said. He sounded like he was hovering around rejection – so my dad risked intervention. It was a moment of pure inspiration, my dad told me. One of those rare instances when you actually say what you're usually left wishing you had afterwards.

'There's a huge difference between my brother and

Lowry,' he interjected. The gallery owner looked a little startled. 'Lowry was an outsider looking in at the world he painted. But my brother, he paints from the inside. Those figures in Lowry's paintings – he's one of those people. And his work is saying something completely different.'

It's often wrongly assumed, I think, that Lowry was working class – based on the subject matter of his paintings and perhaps just the fact he was from the north. But his upbringing was quite middle class – his father was a clerk at a property company and he grew up in the leafy Manchester suburb of Victoria Park.

Following my dad's appeal, the gallery owner took another look at the work, and my uncle, and agreed to take the paintings. My dad told me this was the one time he felt his brother truly appreciated his involvement. That assessment seems a little tough but it's not without justification. My uncle veered between two extremes in his attitude to my dad. To others he was his greatest champion, effusing about his younger brother's charisma and movie star good looks, with touching sincerity – and some delusion, at least on the latter. But frequently, in their actual day-to-day interactions, my dad could do no right, his every suggestion greeted like an affront to basic common sense. My dad, I think, would have appreciated a little less of both.

Eric now had three of his paintings for sale in perhaps Manchester's leading fine art gallery. You might assume he'd be elated. But in fact, somewhat unbelievably, he left the gallery aggrieved. The seeds of the relationship's undoing had already been sown. As soon as he was alone with my dad, he began grumbling about the gallery's commission – which my dad assured me was no more than standard. 'Bloody hell, I do all the work!' Eric protested, as if already jaded by an arrangement that was minutes old. My dad tried to persuade him that having a percentage of something was better than having all of nothing. But this argument saw my dad relegated from his brief status as part of the solution back to being part of the problem. One of 'them'.

The details of what happened next are hazy. Eric returned to the gallery two or three weeks later. Two of his paintings had sold, which should have been a cause for celebration. But despite this, the gallery owner didn't want to take any more. Though perhaps my uncle also didn't press him to, given his distaste for the arrangement. The third painting returned home with him, quite possibly withdrawn from sale at his request. It wouldn't be the only time. Decades later, my aunt – who, like my dad, tried to encourage her brother – arranged for a couple of his paintings to be placed in a small gallery near her home in Oxfordshire. He duly handed over two pictures. But not long after this, and without explanation, he instructed her to get them back.

Eric's encounter with the Tib Lane Gallery seemed to show that he just couldn't be helped. He was his own worst enemy. As soon as he'd secured an opportunity, he was unhappy about it, unable to make peace with the fact that, obviously, the gallery takes a cut. I think whatever that percentage had been, it's unlikely he would have felt comfortable with it. This wasn't really about money, it was about trust. After such a long run-up at approaching the gallery, what had soured things for him so quickly?

He'd surely felt vulnerable offering his work up for assessment, as most artists do. Though that seemed particularly fraught for my uncle who'd had to dredge up his confidence from rock bottom. Likely he'd felt disheartened that the gallery owner had required some persuading to accept his paintings. More specifically, perhaps he'd felt that the dealer's hesitancy was more about him than his work. It might explain why the dealer didn't want to take any more paintings, despite two selling. If, in fact, it was as simple as that. Because regardless, my uncle was entirely capable of generating these feelings himself. He had, I think it's fair to say, extraordinary trust issues.

It was one of his great paradoxes: he loved people. But he was often mildly suspicious of seemingly anyone who wasn't a close blood relative. And extremely suspicious of institutions, private enterprise, anyone professional, anyone to the right of Tony Benn, or who didn't respond to the comedy of Ken Dodd. Those were the rules on paper, but they could be wildly flouted: for example, he was very fond of my brother's *Telegraph*-reading in-laws. And a family member could just as easily fall under suspicion as a total stranger.

It wasn't a pleasant feeling – to be reminded that he didn't exactly trust you. I remember I once placed a bet for him online. We were at my aunt's house in the countryside and he couldn't get to the bookie's. I made a point of talking him through the whole process as I tapped away on my phone: navigating my way to Betfred's website, setting up an account, entering my card details, finding the race meeting, and placing the bet. 'If you need a tenner from me, Joseph, just ask – you don't need to go through all that,' he deadpanned as he handed me his cash. I laughed, but we both knew the joke smuggled a nugget of truth.

Where exactly this chronic mistrust came from, I wasn't sure. It was liable to be triggered anywhere he felt uncomfortable, outside of his own world. The gallery was prime territory for it. 'You've gotta watch these buggers.'

My dad believed that the rejection by the Tib Lane Gallery – the gallery owner's lack of interest in taking more work – had hurt his brother, though he never spoke about it. Whatever the case, the whole experience seems to have put him off ever bothering to seek gallery representation again. The cost was too high, and I don't just mean the gallery's commission. But it didn't appear to have discouraged him one bit in his art-making, as far as I could see by the evidence he left behind. His rate of production looked entirely unaffected. And there were no concessions to making his work more marketable – he continued to indulge his usual preoccupations.

My dad told me that he feels guilty that he didn't or wasn't able to do more, during his brother's life, to help him with his art. But I think he can take some comfort from this episode. On closer enquiry, the effort doesn't seem as unsuccessful as it must have felt at the time. It meant that my uncle got to hear my dad's impassioned defence of his validity as an artist – words that might not otherwise have been spoken, and a sense that the world as he experienced it can't have provided: that the perspective he was painting from – as an uneducated, working-class man – wasn't a disadvantage, but a part of what made him unique and his work authentic.

It often seemed like my dad could barely open his mouth without Eric claiming he'd erred in the most basic fashion. They disagreed over almost everything. But my uncle valued his younger brother's opinion above all others, particularly when it came to art. My dad's words that day in the gallery were a sizeable shovel of fuel, I'm sure, to the fire that kept my uncle painting – that kept him following his instincts – for all the years that followed. It may have been as much as my dad could do to help his brother; it may have been as much as his brother needed.

CHAPTER 5

WHAT'S OUR ERIC DOING THERE?

In the summer of 1996, when I was fourteen, my grandad Bert died. He was seventy-six and in hospital with a punctured lung, the result of years spent working in a chemical factory without adequate protection.

Here's a thing worth mentioning about my grandad. Though he was my dad and Eric's stepfather, and I called him Grandad, he was actually my great-uncle. I know that sounds like a revelation in a soap opera, but the reason, I promise, is fairly banal – my dad first met my mum because she was his stepfather's niece. Bert was her uncle.

My mum took me to see him in hospital shortly before he died. His condition deteriorating, he'd been moved to a private room. He was lying unconscious, his small, slight frame on a giant hospital bed, his dark hair, usually slicked to his head with pomade, revealing itself to be surprisingly long. Me being an awkward teenager, unsure what to do, my mum suggested I take his hand lying palm open at his side. I did this and his hand closed around mine, holding it tightly. I felt a rush of emotion as it seemed he knew I was there and why. Leaving the hospital, I felt a heavy pang of regret that I hadn't been able to know this man quite as closely or as freely as I would have liked. The tension and lines of separation in King George Crescent, which I'd mostly been oblivious to, suddenly felt very palpable. It was strange and alien to me to feel some resentment – some anger even – towards my uncle.

My grandad's death finally brought an end to an unresolvable tension that had lasted nearly half a century. Though that hardly seemed fair – because it was difficult not to see Eric as the cause of it all, as the son who had failed to leave home. Over the decades they were married, my grandparents had little time solely in each other's company. There were the summer holidays Eric spent with us in Pembrokeshire, plus a handful of occasions they went away without him, on coach trips or to visit friends. It doesn't amount to a lot in a fifty-year marriage. Following his stepfather's death, my uncle got what he had always appeared to want, strange as it is to say: unimpeded access to his mother.

Eric was her devoted companion. He kept her in good spirits and took her on runs out in his car. He did the weekly grocery shop, which he aimed to complete just before the supermarket was officially open but when, he'd discovered, the doors were unlocked. He looked after the house, trying to keep it tidy to his mother's standard. This was the only real point of disagreement between them as my grandmother fought to limit my uncle's hoarding. Over the years, according to Eric, his mother had thrown out untold items he'd collected that would now be worth a fortune. These included several complete collections of cigarette cards and an old book in Gothic blackletter that he'd found during a building site clearance – items of such pricelessness, in my uncle's mind, that they would have broken the *Antiques Roadshow*. Even here though, he kept his complaints strictly in good humour, conscious never to upset his beloved mother.

Every week, he brought her to my parents' house for Sunday lunch. The routine was the same each time. My mum would make a roast dinner. My nanna would drink a glass of sherry, my uncle a Guinness. He would give me a CD or DVD he'd received free that week with the *Mirror*. Without fail, one would be handed over: *The Hits of Jerry Lee Lewis*, *Cardio Burn Workout*, *Two Classic Episodes of Open All Hours* – I amassed an eclectic collection. Sometimes things got much more colourful. Occasionally, after lunch, Eric would regale us with stories of his social life – of freewheeling, picaresque adventures lubricated by alcohol. These stories brought him to life, as if telling them were like drinking some fortified tonic that stirred every cell. They were decades old, from a time in his life before the Tib Lane Gallery episode, when Eric was in his thirties and forties. But they felt, as he told them, like much more recent events.

They sometimes took in venues that my parents knew, though with a sense that they'd only skimmed the surface of these places, whereas my uncle had wrung them dry. Generally, they described exploits beyond the scope of your average socialiser, augmented by Eric's aversion to making plans or using the telephone. He would travel as far as Brighton without first making a single enquiry at a boarding house. This reduced his choice of 'digs' – sought on arrival – to the least popular and worst establishments. And if they were full, he slept on the beach. He would set off somewhere, meet a guy he knew on the train, lose him in a pub and then bump into another friend later – or else make one.

Much later, I came to appreciate this was a part of his art-making, providing source material. Or at least it all sprang from the same zest for a certain kind of life. I was also struck by the contrast between the man in these stories, and the man telling them, sat next to his mother on my parents' two-seater sofa, holding her walking stick between his knees. It was another of my uncle's great paradoxes. He was a highly sociable character – most of his art chronicles the social life of his community – but also a very solitary figure. I realised I'd never met any friends of his during his life, except for Mr Hassan, his friend from Betfred, right at the very end of it. Buller I first met at his funeral. How had this rambunctious socialiser ended up with only his elderly mother for close company? And why did these experiences mean quite so much to him?

There was one friend of my uncle's I could name, though he'd died many years earlier and I'd never met him. But he regularly cropped up in my uncle's Sunday-afternoon anecdotes: Adge. Short for Harry and pronounced like 'edge' – which is fitting.

Adge, according to Eric's gleeful description, was 'stone mad' and 'a master at getting out of trouble'. He was a tallish man, bald on top with slicked-back, silvery-dark hair at the sides and an impressive handlebar moustache. My parents had met him once or twice. He was scary, my mum said. Adge had been a Japanese prisoner of war, an experience that my uncle believed had robbed him of fear and any sense of responsibility for the consequences of his actions. (I suspect, conveniently, this also allowed my uncle not to hold him responsible: it wasn't Adge's fault but the Imperial Japanese Army's.) A decade older than my uncle, Adge was married with children – though this proved no barrier to him joining my uncle on nights out. Adge, by his very nature, could not settle down.

They worked together at Monk's building company. Adge was a lorry driver and my uncle would go out on deliveries with him. In mid-life, they became firm friends. Their work and social life blended into one another – sometimes to terrifying effect, as Adge would drink several pints before getting behind the wheel of their twenty-tonne low-loader. On one such occasion, my uncle told us, Adge took a roundabout far too fast, sending one of the giant wooden drums of coiled cable they were transporting bouncing off down the road behind them. In such incidents, Adge was immune to repercussions, my uncle said. In fact, he actively taunted fate. On another occasion, while Adge was driving inebriated, they approached a police officer directing traffic. My uncle instinctively shrunk in his seat but Adge wound down his window and proceeded to start a conversation with the officer – for no other reason than sheer relish of the risk.

A regular trick of theirs, my uncle told us, was to insert a night out into their delivery schedule, claiming afterwards there'd been some unavoidable delay. En route to their destination, they'd hide the lorry in a dimly lit backstreet of whichever town or city they were passing through before hitting its pubs and clubs. Then they'd try to sleep off the worst of their drunkenness in the lorry's cab before continuing on their way. On an occasion when my uncle wasn't with him, Adge awoke from one of these naps to discover his entire load had been stolen. Several tonnes of building site supplies and heavy machinery had vanished while he slept soundly just a few feet away. How, in a journey with no planned stops, would Adge explain this to his employer? But somehow, impervious to consequences as ever, he lived to see another day on the job.

One Sunday afternoon at my parents' house, I filmed Eric telling his stories for a school project. I dug out the video and rewatched it – the only footage we have of him. In it, he takes us through a typical night out in Manchester with Adge. Their haunts were the city's roughest dives – long since-demolished venues such as Tommy Ducks, a pub which, in a disconcerting mix of chauvinism and the macabre, had ladies' underwear hanging from its ceiling and coffins for tables. One reportedly contained a real skeleton. Also, Liston's Music Hall – something of an unofficial gay bar, hosting female impersonators and a swearing parrot on the bar. And the nearby Yates's Wine Lodge, then a 'spit-and-sawdust saloon' serving 'blobs', a potent mix of Australian white wine, cheap brandy and lemon juice.

After an evening's drinking in these venues and more besides, Adge's mind would turn to curry. He was a prolific eater who could 'shift half a ton of the stuff', my uncle explains. They would take a taxi to Adge's favourite Indian restaurant where the owner, Mr Kazi, welcomed Adge in like an old friend. 'Give this man whatever he wants!' he would tell his staff as he showed them to their table. My uncle shakes his head as he tells us this, delighting in the mysterious alchemy of Adge's effect on Mr Kazi. Perhaps it was recognition of a kindred spirit because Mr Kazi was also, according to my uncle, 'a madman'. Sometimes as they sat eating, he explains, a member of staff would break free from the kitchen in an explosion of shouting, then run for his life through the restaurant, closely followed by Mr Kazi wielding a cleaver. This being a semi-regular occurrence, the clientele would hardly lift their eyes from their plates.

Once Adge had had his considerable fill of chicken balti and pilau rice, they'd 'go and do a club', Eric tells us. It was generally around two o'clock in the morning by this point and licensed venues were closed, so Adge and my uncle would head for the 'shebeens' – the illicit bars – of Moss Side. This was exactly the kind of material, by the way, that I was looking to get on camera as a teenage documentarian. These shebeens were all-night, unlicensed drinking dens, hidden behind the doors of ordinary terraced houses and generally operated by and for members of the local Caribbean community. There'd be a bar in the living room, my uncle explains, with settees arranged around it. There were no lights on and they had no idea what they were drinking. But they'd continue drinking it until around five o'clock in the morning when Adge – his great appetite stirring once again – would suggest breakfast. And by this, he meant returning to Mr Kazi's restaurant, though Mr Kazi was now much less enthusiastic to see him. Adge would knock on the door of the restaurant – a heavy, solid wood job with a small slot in it that Mr Kazi would slide open and peer through. 'Bloody hell, not again!' he'd curse on seeing them at this ungodly hour. But nonetheless, he would let them in and feed them another substantial serving of curry and rice.

Frequently these nights out in Manchester ended in disarray. On one occasion, Adge – an incorrigible pursuer of women, despite his marriage vows – unwittingly went home with a cross-dressing man. 'I didn't know, Eric,' my uncle reports his friend soberly telling him afterwards. 'Nice apartment,' he'd apparently added as a strangely wistful detail. On another occasion, Adge staggered onto the wrong train home and woke up in London. Though this was preferable to the time when, insanely, Adge drove the pair of them home – and sent the car sailing into the metal signage in the middle of a roundabout, putting both men in hospital; an act which, incredibly, didn't end the friendship.

Eric obviously considered the rewards of knowing Adge worth the risks. It wasn't this way for others. Adge's long-suffering wife eventually left him. And there were just four people at his funeral, my uncle mentions in the video: my uncle, Adge's brother and two sons. In the end, the consequences caught up with him. Like my uncle, it seems Adge also suffered a dearth of close relationships. Perhaps this was part of what drew the two men into each other's orbits. Both were unwilling or unable to live a conventional middle-aged life. Both had misfit energy. In Adge's case, my uncle put it down to the trauma of war. But where did it stem from in his own life?

My uncle sincerely admired his friend, I think, as a

singular, uncompromising character; a man afforded no power by the world who had a power of his own making. He was a conduit to the kind of adventures my uncle craved. Though in these, my uncle was half-participant, half-observer. Adge, on the other hand, was all in.

Another favourite topic of Eric's, on Sunday afternoons, was a pub called the Forresters Arms. The Forresters was about twenty miles from his house, on the east road out of Manchester towards the Peak District, in the working-class suburb of Openshaw. It was run by relatives: my grandad Bert's older brother, Fred, and his partner, Lily. Being on the far side of a big city, the Forresters was a little wilder and weirder than the pubs of Warrington, but more homely than venues in the city centre – not least, for my uncle, given the family connection. His trips to Manchester often culminated in taking the bus out east to visit the place. It seemed to provide him with something vital.

The pub's clientele was particularly colourful by Eric's reckoning, largely drawn from the surrounding streets with the occasional visitor from the moors to the east. He recalled one such regular, a fierce-looking man who would call in for his pint with a row of dead stoats and weasels dangling from his belt. My uncle also liked to reminisce about the Forresters' in-house pianist – a woman with the hands of a heavyweight boxer, he claimed, and a voice deepened an octave by chain-smoking; neither of these facets hampering her in regularly leading the pub in a rousing chorus.

This great love of character is clear in Eric's paintings, particularly his pub pictures. His work can appear to verge on caricature but I think it's a mistake to see it that way. His characters are larger than life, certainly, but I think he felt that so-called ordinary people very often were larger than life, that working-class life was richer and more vital than commonly appreciated. My uncle's favourite characters at the Forresters – the proprietors themselves, Fred and Lily – were perfect examples of this.

Fred, like my grandad, was a small, slight man – so small, according to my dad, that he looked almost dwarfish. Energetic and affable, he was the front-of-house host while Lily – who my uncle claimed was twice Fred's size in height and width – was the businesswoman in the arrangement. She was the landlady – it was her name over the door.

Every evening, Lily could be found perched on a stool behind the bar, smoking, occasionally rising to operate the till while Fred zipped around serving drinks. During the daytime, she did the bookkeeping from her bed. My uncle recalled once seeing this: Lily in her nightie, ledger in hand, surrounded by bundles of cash, a cigarette stuck to her bottom lip drizzling ash onto the bedclothes. Balancing the books at the Forresters was a delicate operation. Not everything that passed through the pub could be easily accounted for – more on which shortly.

Despite my uncle's tensions with his stepfather, Fred and Lily welcomed him in as family. Occasionally, he even stayed over. My grandmother told us she would roll her eyes on learning that her son had, once again, made his pilgrimage to the Forresters. 'What's our Eric doing there?' she would wonder, oblivious to the appeal. I asked my parents, how had Eric gotten to know Fred and Lily so well? My mum shrugged. 'Through drinking in pubs.' The same way everybody knew everybody.

Fred and Lily both liked a drink – something of a mixed blessing when you run a pub. Despite his stature, Fred would sink a pint in one, graceful movement, picking up the glass full and returning it to the table empty. While Lily, in her dotage, kept a silver teapot of whisky by her side to top up her cuppas. After her death, her broom cupboard was found to be filled floor to ceiling with the empty bottles.

Before running their own pub, Fred and Lily had worked in the bars and hotels of Blackpool and it was here they had first won a place in my uncle's heart. Visiting the seaside resort one summer with a friend, Eric called in at a hotel just off the seafront where Fred and Lily were working, then as later with Fred serving tables and Lily at the till.

Fred, the consummate host, introduced my uncle and his friend to a table of girls and proceeded to take everyone's order. Then he turned to my uncle for payment. In silent horror, my uncle handed over his cash – practically everything he had for the night. But when Fred returned with the drinks and pushed my uncle's change into his hand, he realised he was holding more cash than he'd paid with. And so the evening went on – with my uncle paying and Fred plying him with enough change to keep buying rounds all night.

This one act endeared Fred and Lily to Eric irrevocably.

And thanks to his gift for retelling it, it helped raise Fred and Lily to near-mythical status in our family. They ran the Forresters in much the same spirit. There was little acknowledgement of the licensing law's opening hours. Lock-ins were a regular occurrence, my uncle told us, with service starting as soon as Fred was awake and in the bar and continuing for as long as he could stay there.

My uncle noticed that Fred and Lily were also running another line of business from the premises, trading an eclectic mix of items all stashed behind the bar. He'd seen Fred produce everything from raw meat to a full-sized bicycle from under the counter, handing them to customers in between pulling their pints. Sometimes the police would raid the premises, though mysteriously they never found anything. Perhaps because, as my uncle had noticed, at least one of the raiding officers was a regular at Fred and Lily's lock-ins. Their trade in (presumably) stolen goods only served to enhance Fred and Lily's status as loveable rogues. They were crooks but, crucially, they were crooks with a heart – which placed them high in my uncle's moral hierarchy, above mugs and real crooks.

Like much of the world Eric inhabited, the Forresters Arms no longer exists. I tracked its disappearance on Google Street View. In 2014, it appeared to still be open. An enigmatic poster in the window reads 'PAUL'S BACK THIS FRIDAY'. But a year later, the signage is gone and there's graffiti on the door. Then eventually, a Thai massage shop and a hair salon occupy the space where once Fred and Lily hosted the characters of Openshaw and beyond.

Eric often seemed impervious to his world disappearing. For him, it remained alive. Possibly, it now occurs to me, because he spent so much time in his painting room mentally dwelling there. I sometimes experienced this phenomenon directly. He would tell me to visit Oldham for a proper night out where, he assured me, I'd find a 'turn' on in every pub. And when I first moved to London, he insisted I should visit a pub called Dirty Dick's. 'Haven't you heard of it? It's world-famous!' he barked, concerned at how little I knew of the city I was planning to call home. He explained how an old curse meant the pub could never be cleaned. I could look forward to seeing all kinds of things stuck to the walls by visitors capitalising on this rule, including a dead cat. Unsurprisingly, I never sought the place out. But from the way my uncle spoke, it never occurred to me that it didn't still exist. Then one day I found myself in an entirely sanitary pub in east London and, glancing down at the bar menu, I suddenly realised I was there. I looked around the unremarkable, pleasantly furnished bar. Never had I imagined feeling strangely wistful not to find a dead cat nailed to a wall.

On reflection, there's a strong sense in his stories of Eric as a solo traveller – even with Adge, of two loners flying in tandem. I asked my dad about his brother's social life before this time. In his twenties and early thirties, he was part of a close-knit gang, my dad remembered, which included Buller. They drank at a pub in town called the Cross Keys. This crumbling Victorian ale house still stands, though it's now closed and looks marooned opposite a Brutalist office complex and the back of a big Asda.

My dad was also a regular. He had a separate group of friends from his older brother but they were all part of the wider Cross Keys crew. It was a real fraternity – they looked out for one another. When my dad was in hospital with tuberculosis, they dispatched pints of Guinness to his bedside. And through collective ingenuity, they once successfully removed a patron's rotten tooth in the bar.

They went on day trips, my dad said: 'the darts team' – a term giving a thin veil of officialdom to what really meant all the regular drinkers – plus Joe the landlord who also joined these outings. The destination would be somewhere providing a smorgasbord of drinking opportunities: Rhyl or Blackpool, for example. Everyone turned up at the pub first thing in the morning, to get a pint in before the coach arrived at ten. The coach company, correctly assessing the tone of the excursion, would send their most dilapidated vehicle. On one occasion, my uncle climbed on board to find a large hole in the floor, through which he could see the driveshaft and the tarmac of the road racing past as they went on their merry way. En route, they would call at a pub or a working men's club for another drink or two, my dad explained to me. They'd be welcomed like passing pilgrims, with Joe going behind the bar to pull pints. Then it was off to their final destination for the serious drinking to begin.

The Cross Keys shows that a pub in a working-class community was more than just a dispensary of alcohol. It was a community centre, in the truest sense – a coterie of comrades, a second family even. Though let's not get too sentimental about that. My dad mentioned how, often on these day trips, like a troop returned from battle, not everyone would make it back home. 'We left Jackie Kirk in New Brighton,' he said, shaking his head wistfully. 'Broke his leg at the fairground.'

Eric was a mainstay at the Cross Keys, something of a pub legend by his friend Buller's account. 'He was one of only four men in the world who could chin a bar one-handed,' Buller told me, miming a pull-up with his right arm. How Buller had ascertained that statistic in the pre-internet age, and how reliable it was, didn't seem to matter so much as how sincerely he believed it. Telling me stories of their pub antics, Buller mentioned an occasion when a man of short stature had squared up to my uncle, warning him – with what feels like a line destined to fail – that 'dynamite comes in small packages'. My uncle lit a match, Buller said, and threw it at the man, quipping, 'Well, I didn't see you explode.' Buller chuckled to himself, enjoying the memory of this little barside victory. Then his face grew more serious as he remembered something else. One night in the Cross Keys, Buller – who by this time had a young family – lost track and spent his whole week's wages at the bar. My uncle gave him his own pay packet to take home to his wife, telling his friend to 'pay me back as you go'.

'That's the kind of man Eric was,' Buller said solemnly.

It was altogether a very different picture of Eric's social life – and of Eric. He was part of a gang, itself a part of a wider group. A bachelor rolling from job to job, he was much the same as his friends; even enjoying a good degree of status – as a tough guy, a barside wit, a loyal pal. But as, like Buller, his friends began to settle down, get married and have kids, the differences began to emerge. A little later, my dad remembered, his brother had a friend called Georgie who, like him, was a confirmed bachelor. They went to race meetings together. But then Georgie got married too, relatively late in life, effectively ending the friendship.

Around this time, Eric began to do something that also set him apart from his peers: he began to draw in pubs. When exactly he began, we don't know. But, as evidenced by the huge number of drawings we found in his house, it became a compulsion. My dad witnessed him working like this on a couple of occasions. I saw it just once when he took me to the pub one day as a child. He kept scraps of paper and pencils in his jacket pocket. Parked in a corner with a pint, he held his pencil and paper just below the tabletop. 'He worked surreptitiously,' as my dad put it. His subjects never knew they were being captured. These sketches were secreted back into his pockets, taken back to his painting room where, we learned after his death as we matched sketches to paintings, he arranged and assembled them into finished compositions. This was his process. The secret painter.

It strikes me that it was a quietly maverick act to begin to draw the places he drank in and the people around him – to move from participant to observer. And given he didn't know any other artists, it was also an inherently lonely choice. I wonder what came first. Did he pick up this practice because he found himself alone, or was it the other way around? Likewise, had he never settled down because he needed a freewheeling life, or did he come to live like this because he'd found himself alone?

Among Eric's things, my dad found something that went some way to answering those questions. It was a letter his brother had written to their mother during the period, in his twenties, when he lived in South Wales. The letter was so upsetting, my dad had squirrelled it away somewhere and promptly forgotten where. In it, my dad said, his brother spoke of his chronic loneliness. So it seems like, rather than something that crept up on him, it was for some reason lodged there from the outset – hidden beneath the banter and the high jinks but destined to emerge.

However, this didn't exactly match with the man who, on Sunday afternoons, regaled us with stories of his shoestring adventures. He was a solitary person – but he didn't seem, to me, a lonely one. Perhaps by then he'd gotten used to it, but I think there was more to it than that. Not like he'd just made his peace with it, but had found value in it. He had mined it for adventure. He'd gone out and found things that sustained and inspired him. And strangely, as a result of being alone, I think he'd come to experience more of a sense of belonging in the world – or at least in his world.

It strikes me that during times in my life when I've been alone, I've almost certainly met more people and been more open to the world. And conversely, when not alone, I've been more likely to receive strangers as strangers. It was my uncle's friends who settled down who, to a large extent, retreated from the world. He had gone out and met it.

In this, his life and his art rolled into one another. He was a great appreciator of working-class culture – he saw that there was a working-class culture, and it was rich and important. He satisfied himself of that. All life was to be found in those pubs. Everything was going on there. The more he looked and the more he painted, the more I think he saw it and cherished it. The more he appreciated it, the more it inspired his work. His world stayed alive for him because, for him, it was so vivid.

On one Sunday afternoon, when Eric and my grandmother were over for lunch, I found myself looking at a painting of his – a watercolour pub scene which hung in my parents' living room. That had made me as likely to critically assess it as the curtains or sofa but, for some reason, that day I actually looked at it. My uncle was sitting behind me with his glass of Guinness. He saw me focus on a character in the background: a lady in profile with her mouth wide open. It was the only time we ever had something like a conversation about one of his paintings.

'She used to come into the pubs in Manchester and sing opera,' he said.

I asked him if he meant she was busking and he looked at me slightly askance.

'No, she'd just come in and sing.'

Like my uncle, this lady had a passion for the arts and nowhere to really take it – so she took it to the pub. But the moment stayed with me for the fact that my uncle could account for a character he had placed in the background of a picture, one of eleven overall. The memory returned to me after we uncovered all of his paintings. It showed just how much life and living was poured into his work. The amount of work we found showed just how much life and living there was to pour.

Of course, the notable absence in Eric's life wasn't friends – which he had. It was a romantic partner – which he appeared never to have had. It was certainly nothing he ever spoke about. To my knowledge, there was no one. Although there was one small clue I had once inadvertently stumbled across that suggested this hadn't always been the case. Writing this book, I was determined to uncover all areas of Eric Tucker's life – to understand the man as fully as possible. And I was well placed to do it. But there's something unnerving about lifting the lid on unknown parts of a cherished relative's life. Who knows what you might find inside? Picking up this most slender trail of breadcrumbs, I confess I forgot to prepare myself for where it might lead.

CHAPTER 6

THE LADY IN THE PHOTOGRAPH

It may have been the first time I really understood the notion of privacy. I was a young child – six years old, at a guess – and, during an invasion of my uncle's painting room, I decided to go through a chest of drawers in there and interrogate him about every item. It's something I would never have done at home – correctly anticipating my mum's outrage – but Eric I viewed as basically chilled-out and on-the-level, an equal with whom there were no secrets. He would have been more than welcome to take a spin through my cupboards, so why not I his?

He stood over me as I plucked objects from the dusty drawers, and patiently explained to me what they were. They were mostly painting-related: tubes of Oleopasto and little bottles of linseed oil. But then I found a stash of old photographs, each no bigger than a playing card and seeming to me impossibly ancient. I took them out one by one for an explanation. There were pictures of his father – my 'real grandfather', he said – in the backyard of their two-up two-down, and the pair of them together on a cold-looking beach with a donkey. And then I plucked out a photograph of a smiling young woman – someone I didn't recognise. He took it from me and, looking at it sadly, he shook his head. 'I messed that one up,' he said and then he placed the photograph back in the drawer and closed it. It seems like everything significant in my uncle's life – pleasant or painful, win or loss, though generally the latter – was saved and archived, usually in this room.

The moment, and my uncle's words, lodged fast in my young memory. It was a shock to see him emotional, to realise he wasn't just a comedian and he didn't just exist for my entertainment. I didn't ask him any further questions – about who the woman was, what he'd messed up, or how. And I also never mentioned the incident to anyone else in my family until after my uncle's death, some thirty years later.

Following his death, it transpired that most of us had stories like this. That we each had our own slender insights, which for the most part we had never shared, into this most mysterious side of his life. My aunt told me that, when she was a child, her mother would sometimes allude to her older brother having been 'badly let down by a girl'. She was never given any further details. Was this, I wondered, the smiling young woman in the photograph?

In attempting to better understand my uncle and piece together the stories of his life, this felt like the most daunting area to broach, the least fair game for investigation. Though potentially fascinating and illuminating, it very much felt like the most private part of his life. It is for anyone, I suppose, but somehow the more so for him. So I embarked on this particular line of enquiry with a faint sense of dread – a sense, it would transpire, that wasn't entirely misplaced. And as I did so, my aunt told me a story which felt foreboding.

It happened on New Year's Eve, 1969. My aunt was

in a car with a group of friends, driving through the streets of Warrington, her friend's boyfriend at the wheel. Glancing out of her window she spotted something so shocking she shouted out involuntarily.

'It's our Eric! With a girl!'

She was sure she'd just seen her older brother walking down the street with his arm around a woman. Her friends were presumably bemused by what was so incredible about this, but the sight was such an anomaly that my aunt insisted they turn the car around. She needed to confirm it – and, crucially, get a good look at the woman. They drove back down the street slowly. Mysteriously, my uncle – if it was indeed him – seemed to have disappeared. Scanning the pavement for any sign of him, with their heads all turned in the same direction, my aunt and her friends failed to see a car that ploughed into the side of them. They spent the first hours of the new decade in hospital, though luckily no one was seriously injured. Still, the tale felt ominous. A cut-and-dried case of curiosity killing the cat. The collision brought a complete stop to my aunt's investigation. She never even asked her older brother if she had indeed seen him that night.

A little while after his death, a friend asked if I thought my uncle could have been gay, wondering, given his generation, if a closeted sexuality might have been behind his lifelong singledom. My answer was no, I didn't think so, but as I said that I realised it wasn't based on much authority. A general sense, I guess, and of course the small photograph of the smiling, young woman. But those two things didn't amount to a whole lot of solid evidence. And as we had recently discovered masses of unseen art stashed around his house, I was primed to re-evaluate all assumptions.

For an apparently heterosexual man of his generation, he seemed to be uncommonly tapped into gay culture. There was his love, for example, of the drag queen Foo Foo Lammar, whose Manchester club he liked to frequent and whose career he had followed since its earliest days – when Frank Pearson, general manager of a waste paper recycling plant, would turn up at the Ancoats Arms in overalls before changing into a wig, high heels and spangly dress. And if anyone referred to gay men for any reason, Eric would immediately and fervently jump to their defence, regardless of whether or not the prompting comment had been antagonistic. 'Some of the best lads I knew in the army were gay!' he would proclaim loudly and slowly. I always took this to be a part of his ardent solidarity with anyone marginalised or oppressed, including but not limited to homeless people, people with disabilities, Jewish people and Scousers – the latter of whom he liked to declare 'the best people in the world!' But then my dad mentioned how his brother would sometimes tell stories, from his time in the army, of the London gay scene. How there was 'a guy at the barracks' who would take soldiers into town to meet men. Men like the film actor Stewart Granger who, my uncle claimed, was in a relationship with one of his fellow Horse Guards. Given that homosexuality was illegal at the time, is it revealing that my uncle was privy to all this? Or was it simply the case, as he claimed, that it was just well known in the regiment?

Another memory occurs to me as potentially relevant. In the 1990s, Eric became obsessed with a local radio host called Allan Beswick. There was almost an element of teenage fandom about the fixation. Our experience of this phenomenon began with occasional mentions of Allan and his afternoon phone-in show when Eric and my grandmother were over for Sunday lunch. As with many of my uncle's anecdotes and reference points, he assumed knowledge on our part, casually referring to 'Beswick' until one of us asked, 'Sorry, who's Beswick?' To which he barked, 'Beswick! Allan Beswick on the radio!' Then he and my grandmother stared back at us from the sofa, perplexed that we weren't familiar with the daytime schedule of BBC Radio Manchester, even though my parents had full-time jobs and I was at high school.

These occasional mentions increased in frequency until, eventually, the phenomenon was in full swing. Every Sunday we got a detailed account of that week's highlights, the show's quirkiest callers, and how Allan had once again proven himself a plain-speaking oracle and bastion of common sense. Eric's adoration of Beswick became a running joke in the family – one my uncle knowingly played up to. Somehow any conversation would eventually come around to Beswick and what his unparalleled take on things would be. Having decided that he and Beswick were in full agreement on all matters, that they were practically of one mind, Eric started to use the presenter as a thinly veiled front for his own frank assessments of our problems. It was a quietly ingenious move. Take issue with my uncle and we were shooting the messenger – he was simply telling us what Allan Beswick would say. And we couldn't really argue with that since we almost entirely experienced this man through the mediumship of my uncle.

My mum was growing increasingly rankled by her brother-in-law's Beswick obsession. Then one Sunday she made the mistake of sharing a predicament in her life. A minor domestic issue but one gnawing at her nonetheless. The details of it are beautifully banal: she had accepted an overpriced quote from a builder to replace a short length of guttering. Having seen the finished job, she had then realised her mistake. She'd asked the builder for an itemised bill. He'd obliged, flagrantly exaggerating how many days it had taken an alleged small army of men to install less than a metre's worth of gutter.

My mum was sharing this little dilemma with everyone, harvesting all opinions, hoping that someone would tell her she was within her rights not to pay in full. And more importantly, that she hadn't been foolish to accept the quote in the first place. Inevitably, it got an airing at Sunday lunch. It was almost painful to witness. My mum even gave a preamble about what a difficult matter this was for her and how she did not – repeat, *did not* – wish to hear what Allan Beswick might have to say about it. But it was futile. This was prime Beswick territory. The builder must've seen my mum coming a mile off – Beswick wouldn't pull any punches in telling her that. My mum looked ready to murder my uncle with the cutlery to hand.

Practically everyone gave her the same advice, though most delivered it more diplomatically than us, her family: that this was her mistake, she'd accepted the quote and it was, unfortunately, time to pay up. But still clinging on to hopes of vindication – and perhaps just eager to shut up my uncle – my mum did something none of us had seen coming. She called in to the Allan Beswick show. She took the matter to the court of Allan one afternoon on BBC Radio Manchester. And it played out as if my uncle had written the script. In the plain-speaking style with which he'd won my uncle's affections, Beswick told my mum that she'd agreed to the quote and she had to pay. Finally, my mum accepted her fate. Beswick had once again worked his magic. It was as if my uncle had brought this man into our lives for real through the sheer force of his obsession.

Years later, when my uncle's ardour for Allan Beswick had waned, he became nearly as fervent an admirer of the chat show host, Paul O'Grady. He was a TV personality beloved of many, but few were more vocal about it than my uncle. O'Grady was spoken of as a near-saintly figure, his many virtues regularly extolled at Sunday lunch. There were no airs or graces about O'Grady.

These fixations had an almost crush-like quality but they were also fitting with my uncle's obsessive nature and his tendency to divide the world into heroes and villains. The villains – Margaret Thatcher, David Cameron – were beyond redemption. The heroes – Allan Beswick, Paul O'Grady – were beyond reproach. Their canonisation was probably indicative of how rarely the media serves up a genuinely working-class voice; my uncle zealously latched on to the few men in public life he felt a genuine affinity with. And that affinity perhaps also reflects the lack of real fellowship in his life at this time.

It wasn't long after the question about my uncle's sexuality was put to me that I interviewed Buller. He mentioned weekends my uncle would spend alone in Manchester. 'Who knows what he was up to,' Buller said, his eyebrows practically twitching. 'I mean, an unmarried man, single – you can just think of anything, can't you?' I wasn't sure if Buller was insinuating something specific. Was he suggesting that my uncle may have been secretly gay? I could imagine this used to be commonly speculated about unmarried men. I mentioned it to my parents but they thought not. 'He probably meant prostitutes,' my mum said bluntly.

This was a whole other arena I hadn't considered. Did my uncle use the services of sex workers? It seems not unlikely. He told us that the doss houses he stayed in with Adge while out making deliveries to building sites were often 'snewin' with working girls'. But ultimately, I didn't fancy ringing eighty-eight-year-old Buller – a man whose deafness made phone calls tricky at the best of times – to ask if he'd meant prostitutes. Listening back to the recording of our interview, it seemed Buller was just wondering aloud about the intriguingly unknowable, hinting that he'd naturally entertained some spicy possibilities. Though never the one that much evidence now pointed to, which hadn't occurred to me either. That my uncle had been spending a good deal of this time in art galleries and creating preliminary sketches for his paintings.

I don't believe my uncle's sexuality was hidden or closeted. If anything, the fact he was unafraid to champion gay rights and enjoy a good drag act seems like evidence of how comfortable he was in himself and his sexuality. Which makes it all the more curious that he didn't more easily express this aspect of himself; that he clearly struggled to form close, intimate relationships.

One reason may be the way he saw himself. He considered himself very ugly. He began to lose his hair in his twenties and this undoubtedly affected his confidence. I noticed in many of his early pencil sketches of boxers and movie stars, the hair was exquisitely rendered, in almost hyperreal detail. But the issue seems to have gone deeper than this. My dad told me that his brother sometimes compared himself to the 'French Angel', Maurice Tillet, a professional wrestler from the 1940s who suffered bone overgrowth and is rumoured to have inspired the look of Shrek. The comparison my uncle made is patently ridiculous but the point, I suppose, is that he was describing how he felt. It occurs to me that he may have suffered from what is now called body dysmorphic disorder.

It seems likely that the young woman in the photograph I found in his drawer was the same girl who had 'badly let down' my uncle. Perhaps this early heartbreak had shattered his already precarious confidence, causing him to swear off romance for a lifetime. With his straggly, self-cut hair and his sellotaped jacket, he seemed to have taken a vow of dishevelment, determined that no one should mistake him for attractive. I had always assumed that he had never been in love. But looking through the paintings he'd left behind, I noticed something. I didn't see it at first. Then it seemed so obvious I couldn't believe I'd missed it.

It was a painting of a jazz club. A relatively late work, by the look of it. A dreamy concoction of a smoky interior with horn players blasting in the background as a singer sashays across the stage. In the foreground, two couples are nestled around tables. But they're not looking at the band or its singer – they only have eyes for each other. For a man who was chronically single, I was suddenly struck by how evocatively he had captured two distinct stages of romantic love: the first glance between one couple, and the deep, adoring gaze of the other. I began to wonder if this could have really only been observed. Or if, in fact, it must have been lived.

My brother told me how, once, when the two of them were alone together on a long car journey to Pembrokeshire – our annual family holiday – and prompted by my brother and his wife expecting their first child, Eric had spoken of his regret that he had never had a family of his own. He briefly alluded, my brother said, to a lost love – someone whom he considered his 'final chance'. The conversation was so out of character that, on arrival, my brother went straight to the pub with his wife to recount what he'd been told. I can understand that impulse. Otherwise, it might have felt like it hadn't happened.

I asked my dad to wrack his brains. Was there anyone he remembered his brother ever having been involved with? There was someone, my dad said. A woman from Yorkshire. He couldn't remember her name.

My dad and his brother, plus a friend of my dad's, had gone on holiday to Paris together for a week one summer in the 1960s. My uncle was in his early thirties. This woman was staying in the same hotel, on the same package trip, and my uncle had taken a shine to her. After the holiday, my uncle went to visit her in Yorkshire – a number of times, my dad told me. His brother didn't give much away, he said, but he thought this relationship had carried on into the early part of the following year – and perhaps even beyond. There was an additional revelation: the woman was married, my dad recalled. Sifting through all the stuff in his brother's house, my dad found two photographs. This was her, he said, handing the pictures to me.

The first photograph was black and white. There were four people sitting around a small table outside a café – a café very much like the one in Van Gogh's *Café Terrace at Night*; a perfectly French scene. My dad's friend Brian, with his arms and legs folded, was sitting awkwardly next to a young woman wearing cat-eye glasses. Across the table from them, my uncle and another woman were sitting close together. She was smiling and she seemed to be speaking. He was leaning in a little and gazing at her. To see my uncle like this was a revelation in itself – looking assured and familiar with a woman, not to mention quite smart. His hair was tidily cropped and he looked positively modish in a fitted shirt and dark tie.

The second photograph was in colour. It was the same woman my uncle had been sitting with in the first picture but here she was alone, reclining along a concrete step. Behind her was the tree-lined boulevard of the Tuileries Garden near the Louvre. She was smiling – laughing even, possibly. Her right hand was holding her left, its forefinger touching something – a wedding ring.

Searching again through Eric's stuff, my dad spotted something else. Towards the back of an old notebook, there was a woman's name in my uncle's handwriting followed by the name and adress of a pub. My dad showed it to me. This, he thought, was her.

I wondered if it might be possible to track this lady down. To find out what her relationship with my uncle had been – if she was the lost love he'd spoken of to my brother. I began to do some cursory googling. The pub, it transpired, no longer exists. Nobody with this lady's surname was listed in the phone book as living in the area and it struck me that this might have been just a place they once arranged to meet. But since there was no time or date in the notebook, it seemed like it was a home or perhaps a work address. And crucially, it was all I had to work with.

I searched the electoral register and the Land Registry's records of the pub's past owners but neither bore fruit. I was beginning to think that if I was serious about finding this woman I might have to turn to a professional. But something about hiring a specialist to track down an old lady felt like crossing a line – one that was already dubiously thin.

So my narrow lines of enquiry appeared to be nearing an end when I started idly reading an article on a local newspaper's website, detailing a councillor's thwarted efforts to prevent the pub from being turned into residential housing. As I got drawn into the tale of a lone man's attempt to throw the council's own planning regulations back in its face, a detail in the story caught my eye. It was the phrase 'Historical Society'. I stopped reading. If anyone was up in the business of a village's residents, I thought, it was its historical society. And if the lady in the Paris photographs was meaningfully connected to this area then these, surely, were the people to call.

I made my way to the group's website and fired off a brief email. Within hours I had a reply from the chairman. And something told me from the tone of his response that he wouldn't let me down; that he understood why I felt this was a job fit for a historical society. The following week he emailed again. He'd found her. I felt a rush of excitement at the news and a flush of reverence towards all village historical societies. She had worked in the pub in the 1960s, he wrote. Someone in the village knew her and they had passed on my number. And so . . . I waited.

Four days later, on a sweltering Sunday in August, my phone lit up with a call from an unknown number. I answered. It was her.

I was aware at this point that I was about to ask a potentially frail old lady details of her private life, and so I should tread very delicately. But I was immediately struck by how vigorous and assured she sounded, apparently quite undaunted to talk about this episode in her life. She knew why I wanted to speak to her, even though I hadn't given any context in my email to the historical society beyond that I was writing a book. But I had included one of the Paris photographs, in case the face jogged any memories where the name didn't. She had recognised the photograph and then my surname. She had even, she said, seen a recent newspaper article about my uncle's artwork and suspected it was the same man she'd met in Paris more than fifty years earlier. I explained how we had found these photographs among his things, plus a notebook with her name and the address of the pub. He kept everything, I said offhandedly. She then wasted little time in telling me, in a matter-of-fact voice enhanced by flat Yorkshire vowels, that her and my uncle's brief association had been 'very romantic for him – but not for me'. My heart broke a little at the thought that this might have been my uncle's one experience of true love. That this could be the woman he considered his 'final chance'.

She had been on holiday with her sister when she met him, she told me. She was in her mid-twenties and married – as my dad had remembered. She and her sister became friends with my dad's trio while staying at the same hotel in Montmartre. One day, she mentioned to the group that she wanted to visit the Louvre and Eric piped up, so did he. And so together they went. Afterwards, he asked if he could hold her hand. And then he kissed her, she said, a little sheepishly.

On another occasion during the week, they'd gone on a shopping expedition together. My uncle asked her to help him choose a gift for his sister, my aunt. She picked out a scarf she thought was nice, he bought it, and then he gave it to her. It had been a ruse to allow him to buy her a gift – one that she didn't sound much moved by. And that was the time they'd spent together in the city, just the two of them. No more than three or four hours in total, she thought. Though then she remembered that on the ferry home she had felt seasick and my uncle had sat with her on deck, in the drizzle, looking after her.

She returned to Yorkshire and to her job at the pub, where she worked part-time behind the bar. And one evening while she was working, not long after the trip to Paris, my uncle turned up at the pub. His arrival was a complete shock, she said. She had never even given him her address, she told me, but he had seen it on her luggage label. 'I never wrote my full address on a luggage label again!' she barked, understandably.

He professed that he was madly in love with her, she said. That he believed it was fate, that they were meant to be together. He asked her to leave her husband for him. She told him that 'this wouldn't do'. That she was married. And again she repeated to me that his feelings towards her were very romantic but hers for him were not.

He presented her with a pair of paintings, she recalled. These would have been two of his relatively early efforts. One was a portrait of the light-heavyweight boxing champion Freddie Mills, she said. The other was a painting of an ornament from his mother's mantelpiece. She found both images, as a gift, 'a bit odd'.

It can't be easy, I thought, to receive paintings of a light-heavyweight boxer and an ornament belonging to the artist's mother as tokens of passion. But they were, I suspected to myself a little sadly, two of the paintings he'd then produced of which he felt proudest. And in a strange way, they were a very honest reflection of the man he was, of the life from which he felt she could liberate him, perhaps. Nevertheless, the whole thing sounded like a quite insane and desperate pitch.

She walked him to the nearest bus station and saw him

back onto the bus, she told me. It's worth noting that the journey by bus from Warrington would have involved several changes and probably took four or five hours, maybe longer. Setting off for home in the evening, the journey back would have surely taken the whole night, with a long layover in Manchester until bus services resumed in the morning. As they said goodbye he was upset, she said, but 'it wasn't over-dramatic'. He told her that he believed they would meet again. He was convinced of it, she said. But after they parted that evening, she never heard from him again. She no longer had the two paintings my uncle had given her, she told me. She had left them in the loft of the house she'd shared with her husband.

I came away from the call with a heady mix of emotions: shock, a little heartache, a sprinkling of panic. That night I slept fitfully. I had a growing feeling that I had uncovered something I shouldn't have. Nothing that ever quite consolidated itself into a rational thought, but just some primordial sense that I'd opened Pandora's box, disrupting the natural state of the universe and somehow displeasing the gods. Also, being met with the outcome of my enquiries had sparked an increasingly inescapable thought that, if nothing else, I'd just done something very odd. Strip away the pretext of writing a book and I had just gone to considerable lengths to track down a lady my dead uncle had once had some kind of affair with, to ask her for the full details. And somehow, her blindsiding willingness to frankly discuss it had only compounded these feelings.

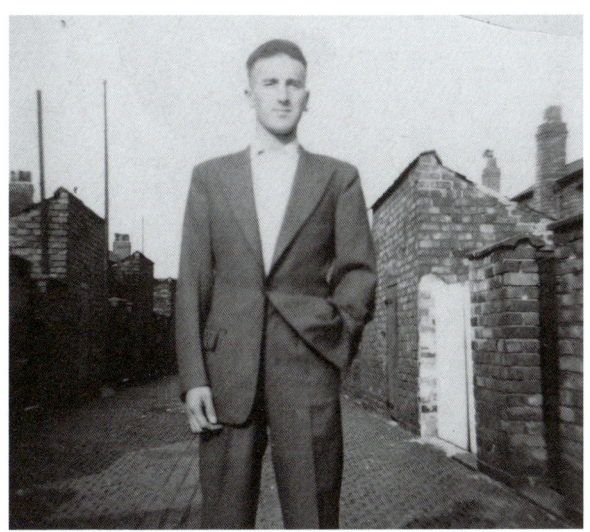

Eric as a sharp-suited young man, in the back alley behind Hume Street, circa 1952.

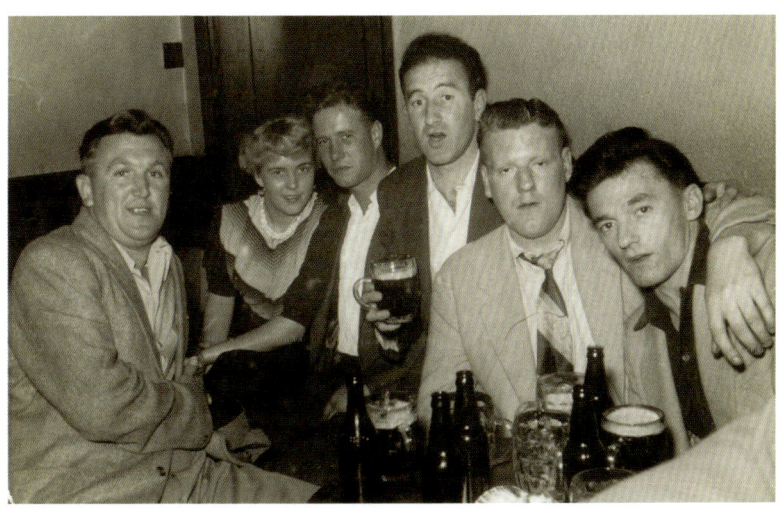

'A tough guy, a barside wit, a loyal pal.' Eric (centre) with his drinking buddies.

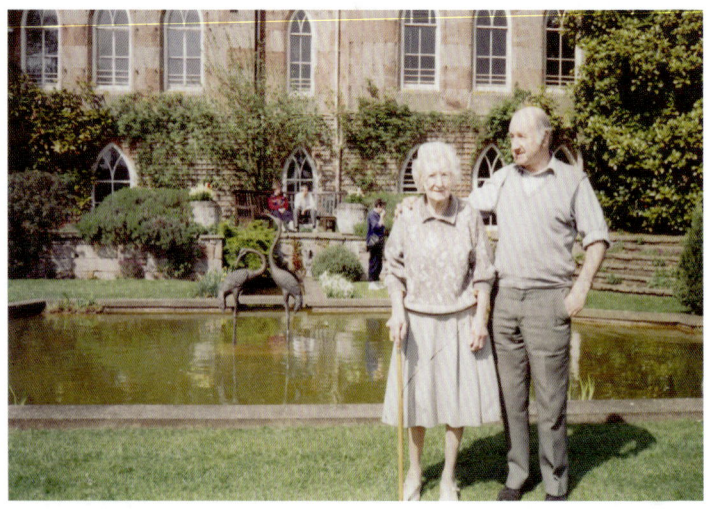

Inseparable: Eric and his mother visiting Cholmondeley Castle in 1994.

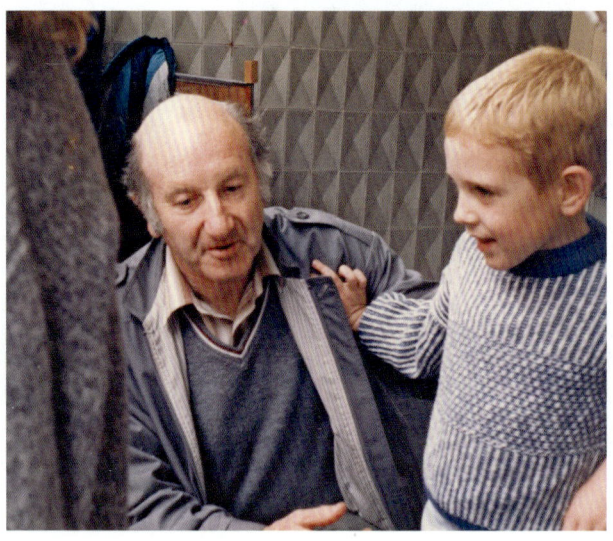

A young me with 'Uncle Eric' – wearing the jacket later to be held together with Sellotape.

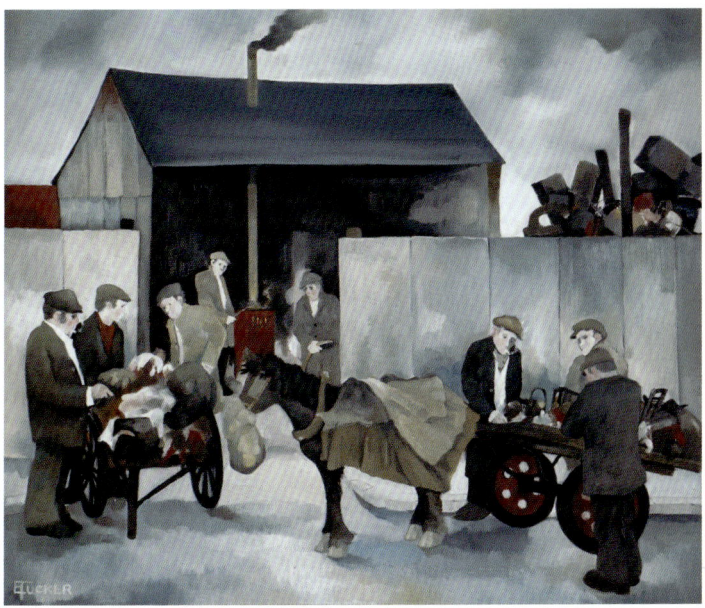

'It was a habit of my uncle's to amass bits of metal scavenged from building site clearances.' (Chapter 4) *Pricing Up at the Scrapyard* (oil on board, date unknown)

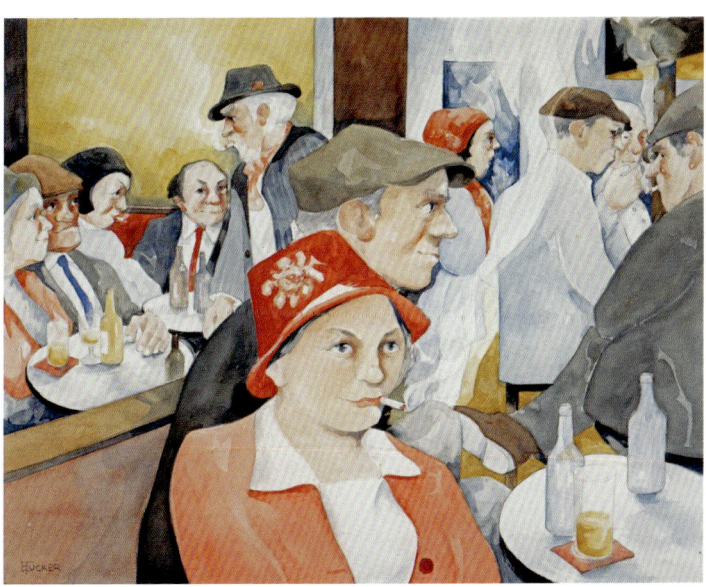

'. . . the moment stayed with me for the fact that my uncle could account for a character he had placed in the background of a picture . . .' (Chapter 5) *City Bar Manchester* (watercolour and pencil on paper, date unknown)

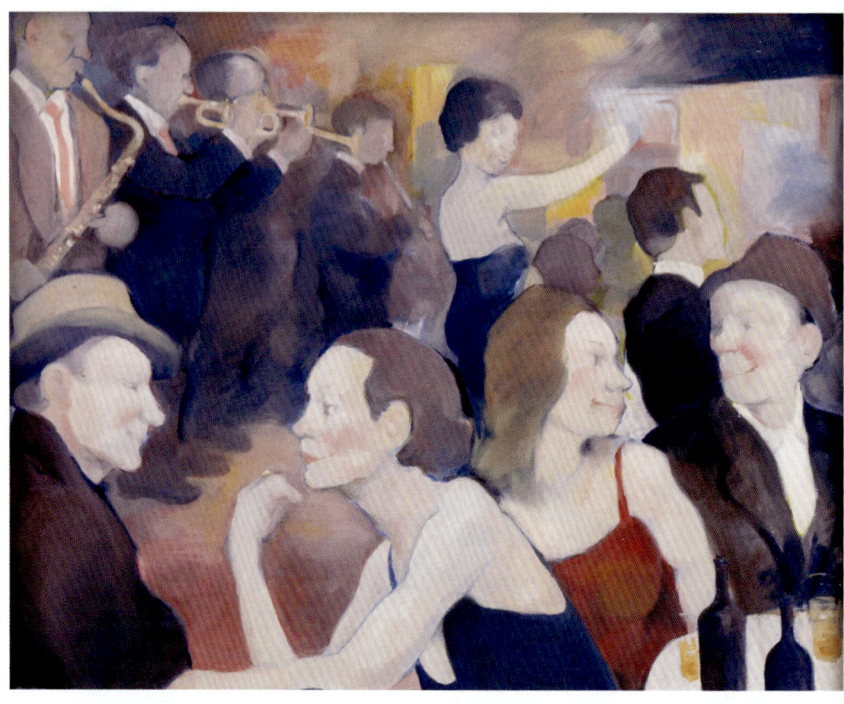

'I was suddenly struck by how evocatively he had captured two distinct stages of romantic love: the first glance between one couple, and the deep, adoring gaze of the other.' (Chapter 6) *Singin' and Swingin'* (oil on canvas, date unknown)

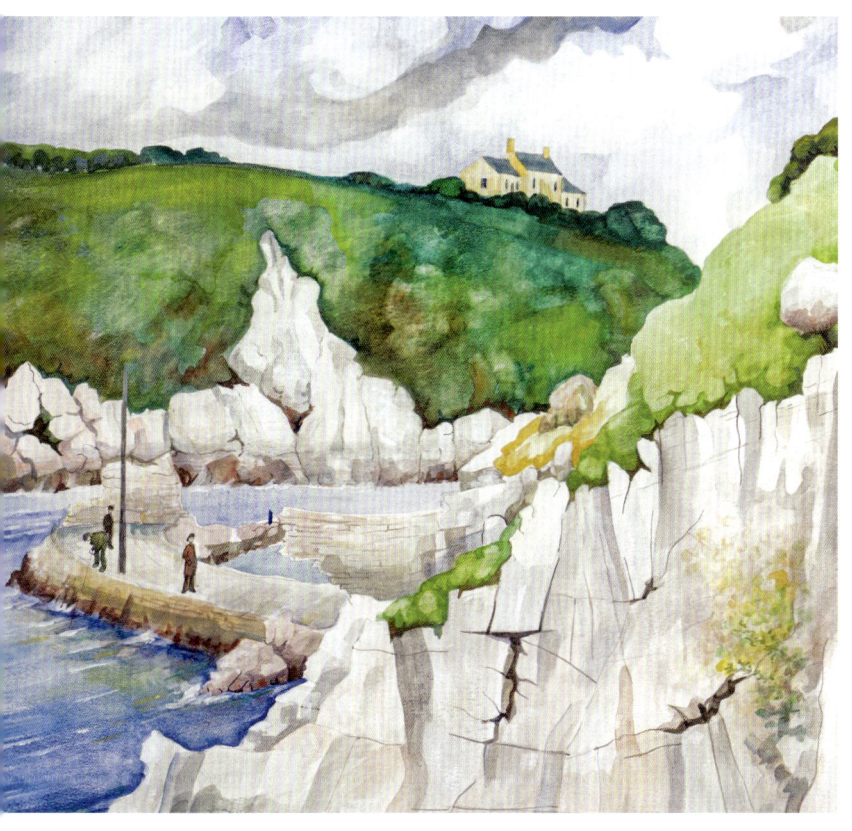

'I was edging precariously towards the surf, but I still hadn't reached the angle of the painting.' (Chapter 8) *Porthclais Harbour* (watercolour and pencil on paper, date unknown)

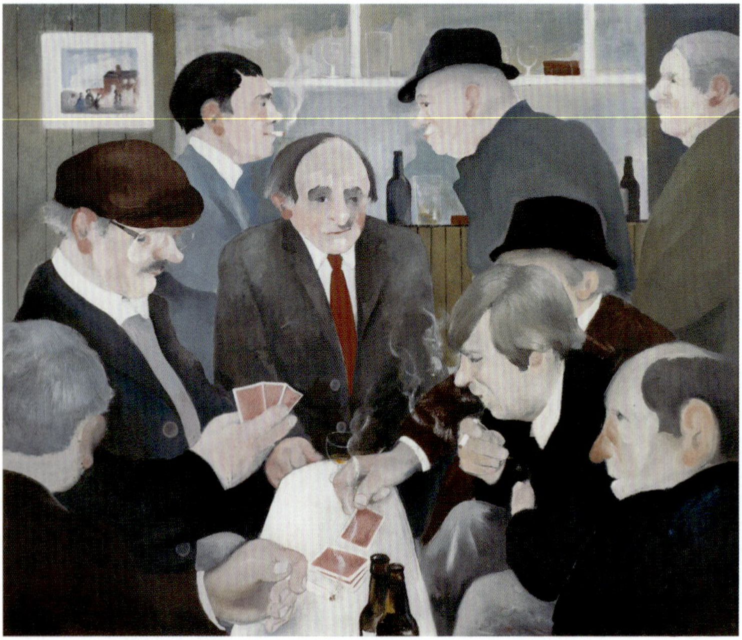

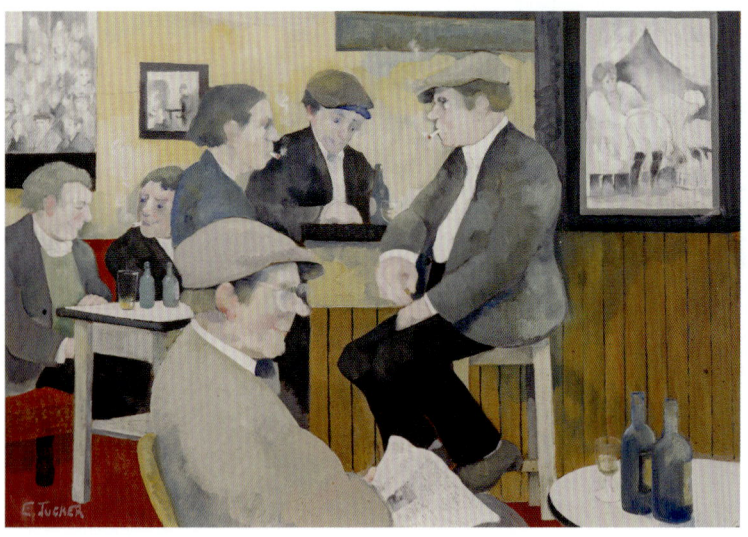

'As I've become more familiar with his paintings, carrying them around in my head, I'll sometimes feel I spot a reference to another artist's work . . .' (Chapter 8) *Card Players* (oil on board, date unknown)

'Some titles required careful thought. Others were decidedly easier.' (Chapter 9) *Bare Arsed* (oil on board, date unknown)

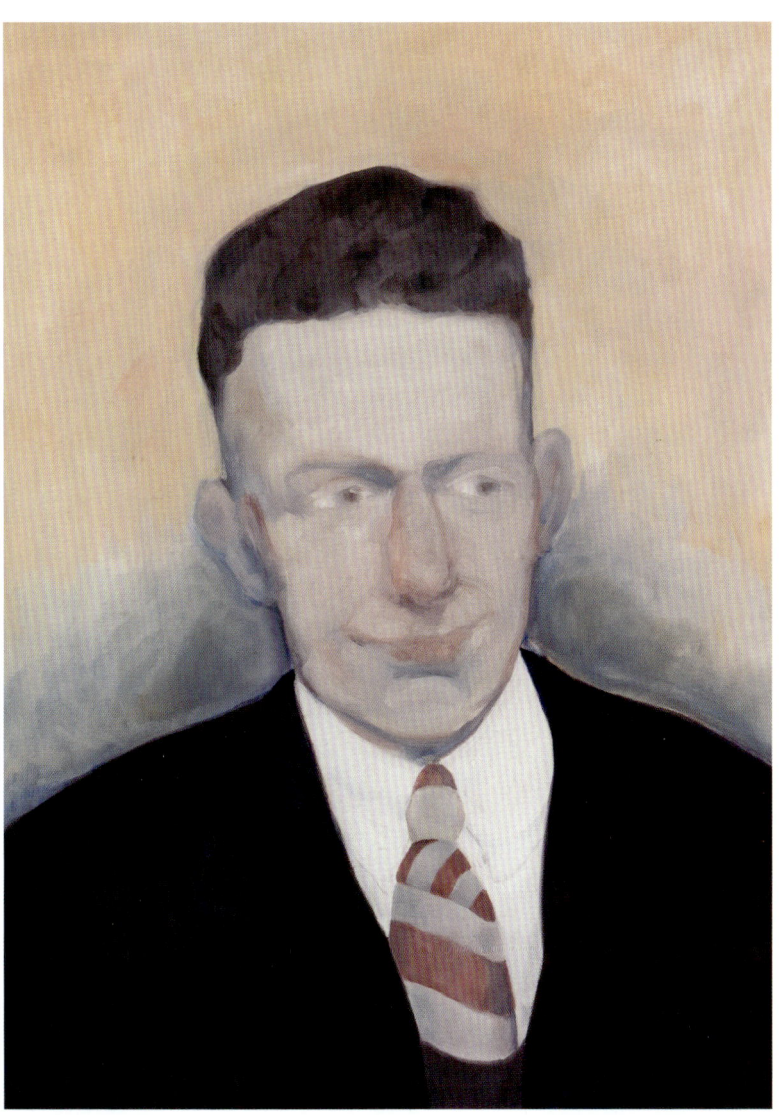

'On the walls, he had hung portraits he'd painted of departed family members . . . It gave the eerie impression that he was preparing to see them again.' (Chapter 9) *Father* (oil on board, date unknown)

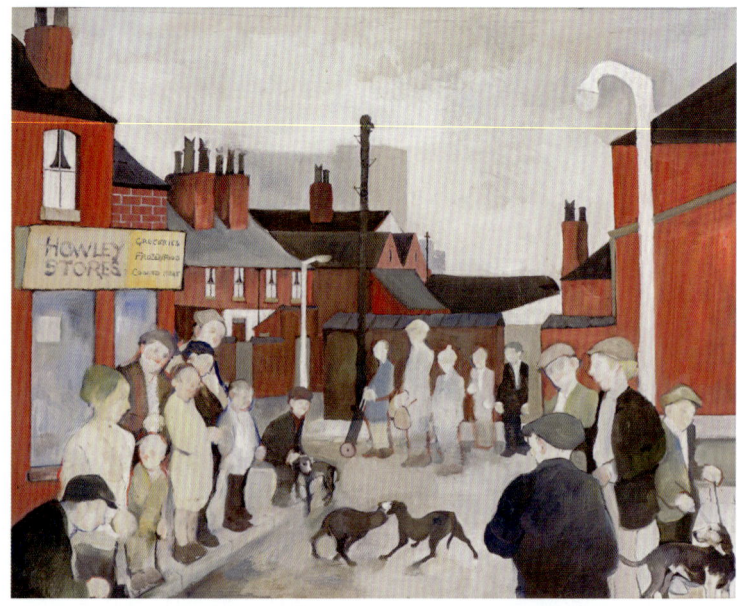

'I could feel my uncle shaking his head at my upbringing, one so gilded it had left me unable to recognise a dog fight.' (Chapter 12)
Fighting Dogs – Howley Stores (oil on board, date unknown)

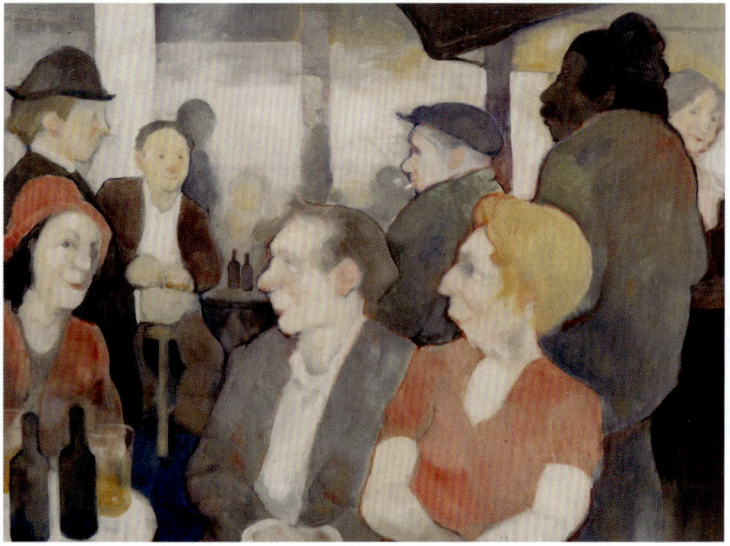

'I'd gone PC mad. I was expurgating the facts! Look at the painting. Here was a bar, and there was a Black man at it!' (Chapter 12) *Redhead and Two Bottles of Beer* (oil on board, date unknown)

But as I regained composure in the light and coffee vapours of morning, I began to wonder about the story I'd been told. I had no specific criticism, but something about it didn't feel quite right. My uncle had apparently been so deeply in love that he had become fatalistic. The strength of his feelings was so consuming that he was convinced they were meant to be together. That sounded like a credible account of a man in the throes of love. But I also wondered, was it really possible he'd developed such deep and fervent feelings inside of a week, with just a few hours' contact, and apparently little reciprocity? Would he really be so bold and emotionally vulnerable as to ask a woman to leave her husband for him with little to reassure him that there might be at least a chance of success? These elements, to my mind, seemed less convincing. But love can cause people to behave in extraordinary ways. Perhaps he was so starved of such experiences that the smallest spark had lit a tinderbox.

There were further questions in my mind. Was it strange that she had apparently written her work address, and not her home address, on her luggage label? And was it just a coincidence that my uncle had turned up at the pub both on a night she was working and, as she had mentioned to me, when her husband wasn't around? These things were possible. But finally, there was the great disparity between this story and my dad's – the fact that he remembered his brother travelling to visit this lady several times over the course of many months.

I called my dad to let him know that I'd spoken to the lady Eric had met in Paris. I told him that she had claimed

Eric visited her just once, soon after their holiday. My dad was confused. He reiterated that he was sure his brother had gone several times, but his confidence seemed to be wavering slightly. My dad doesn't have the most reliable memory. He can sometimes be found staggering around his house exasperatedly searching for the very thing he just put down a moment ago. He has been known to call me by the dog's name. But in recalling these events, he'd correctly remembered such relatively minor details as the husband's job. So was it possible, I wondered, that my interviewee had given me an account of the story which downplayed her participation? I thought about how she had phrased certain elements: he asked to take her hand. Presumably, she let him. Then he kissed her. Presumably, she kissed him back. Perhaps there was more to the story but she feared how it might make her look. But then why bother telling me any story at all? Why bother even calling me?

I remembered something she had said. Right at the end of our call, as I was winding things up, she brought up the fact that my uncle had died a bachelor, which she'd read in the newspaper. She hoped he hadn't spent his life pining for her, she said, before adding, 'But I'm a bit like that – dramatic.' I wasn't quite sure what to say. It felt like a question and I didn't really know the answer. And then she continued in a smaller voice, 'Perhaps, as you said he kept everything, it didn't mean that much.' Again, it felt like she was fishing for an answer. I told her I was pretty sure he'd kept these photographs because they did mean something to him. Was this, I wondered, what she had called to find out?

THE LADY IN THE PHOTOGRAPH

If nothing else, it was a very different tone to the woman who'd bluntly told me that it was 'very romantic for him, but not for me'.

I spoke to her once more, briefly, the following Sunday, to confirm a few details of her story. I told her that my dad was convinced that Eric had gone to visit her a number of times but she insisted it was just the once. Beyond that, I didn't feel like questioning her further – that I had any right to.

Then around five weeks later, I received an email from her. She had dug out a photograph of her own and sent me a picture of it – of herself, her sister, and my uncle together in Paris. The three of them were standing with their arms around one another on some rue or boulevard by the square, stone pillars of a grand old building. My uncle was larking around, gazing up out of frame like an airy figure in a Baroque painting. He looked deliriously happy. The week I received this email, I'd been helping to catalogue my uncle's paintings. A couple of his early efforts had caught my eye as potentially relevant to this chapter of his life. I included photographs of them in my response to her. The first was a painting of an ornament – similar, I thought, to one of the paintings she'd mentioned him giving her. The second was more interesting. It was a painting of a woman in an art gallery, gazing at what appeared to be a loose impression of Van Gogh's 1888 *Sunflowers* – the version which hangs in the National Gallery in London. I compared the woman in the painting with the lady in the Paris photographs – the resemblance was uncanny. I wondered if this could be you, I asked her in my email. I never received a response.

My enquiries had reached the end of the line – though there was one final discovery. I found a letter in a box of my uncle's things. It was from her. Friendly in tone, it was hardly a love letter. But it did seem to contradict the story she'd given me. She was writing, with address provided, to rearrange a visit.

I came to the conclusion that I would never really be sure of what happened in this episode in my uncle's life. In this whole area of his life. So I ended my investigation back at the place I had started, looking at his painting of the jazz club. Perhaps this was the best place to find the answers I was looking for. If the lady in the Paris photographs had been the 'final chance' he had spoken of, if this experience had caused him to abandon any further pursuit of romance, and perhaps even to give up taking much care of his appearance – as the gap between his look when I knew him and the man in these photographs might suggest – then, curiously, I didn't detect the slightest trace of bitterness or regret here, in this painting. Quite the opposite in fact. It seemed to me to be a visceral celebration of falling in love. The luscious colours and the irrepressible music and dancing of it. It was an appealing invitation to attend the club.

CHAPTER 7

WE NEED TO TALK ABOUT NORMAN

As my grandmother reached her nineties, Eric became her full-time carer. Crucially, this meant she could continue living in her own home; something they both seemed to consider essential. My parents had made several cautious attempts to persuade them to move to a soon-to-be-opened retirement village – the kind of facility that caters for all stages of late life. There would be nurses and care staff to supplement my uncle's efforts, and an organised calendar of social events he could tap into. He dismissed the whole idea immediately and fervently. The very notion of a retirement village, through to its glossy brochure, smelled to him like something that could only be the brainchild of a racketeer. It seemed to perfectly trigger his mistrustfulness, his fear of being out of control, and perhaps a concern that it would somehow split him up from his mother.

Rather Eric felt that we, his family – all of us – should be living in the streets surrounding his house. My parents were less than half an hour's drive away, my brother was even closer. Both they and my aunt did much to help him – more in fact than he could often tolerate. This was a position more philosophical than practical. He was disappointed that we didn't live in his world. The younger members of his family had left him behind. The whole world had, to an extent. But I think the way he saw it was more like we'd taken the wrong path. Not with an air of bitterness but a sincere belief that we'd made a bad trade. Or perhaps spoiled the party by leaving it.

For my part, I'd gotten about as far away from home as I could without leaving the country. I'd moved to London. At first, everything about the south-east seemed better by dint of being different. Even the colour of the bricks was thrilling – warm, sunlit shades of yellow as opposed to rain-soaked red. I had left behind small-town small-mindedness for life in a diverse and cultured city.

Then, subtly, some discord began to creep in. I don't mean the tube or the crowds, which everyone hates. I'm talking about a faint feeling of resentment at the theatre, a sense that I'm not quite as pleased to be there as everyone else; a quiet enjoyment of the distress caused by lairy football fans singing on the tube. Matters came to a head when it was revealed a Coral bookmaker's shop would be opening in my area. At the time, I lived in a flatshare in a south London 'village' – a gentrified neighbourhood centred around a quaint street of shops, including a delicatessen, a purveyor of *objets d'art*, and a grocery shop so expensive that, as my flatmate put it, entering felt like visiting a different country where the pound was unusually weak. The news that a bookmaker would be added to this, albeit at the very end of the row, united neighbours – people of all political affiliations – in outrage.

At first, vocal opposition focused on the fact it was a chain business – but the street already had several of these. Hot on the heels of this was a sudden moral panic about the evils of gambling; an issue it was hard to imagine anyone had actively campaigned about before.

Then eventually the uglier truth began to spill out: concern that it would 'draw people up from the wrong end of the street'. Undesirables. The sort who frequent betting shops. And who exactly was that? My uncle, I thought. Suddenly, London didn't seem quite so much the liberal utopia as when I'd arrived.

Around this time, I received a brilliant and unexpected gift from my uncle – a timely disproval of any assumptions about men who frequent betting shops. It was a painting of the view from my childhood bedroom window. Later, following his death, I found a detailed preparatory drawing for it. Nobody had any clue when he could have done it. Receiving the gift, it struck me as so insightful to think what that view would mean to me. Not least because I hadn't realised it myself until I saw it as a painting. He knew the power of home. Characteristically, no words or explanation accompanied the gift. But I've wondered since, was he reminding me not to forget where I was from?

He had an unusually keen sense that the tribe should stick together. So much so that he had never left home, which I think he almost viewed as a valid – even noble – choice rather than a failure. It's a difficult position to make a persuasive argument from. I'm certainly not convinced. Though there are times when, having made a life for yourself in a city away from home, you wonder if it's been worth the cost of slightly estranging yourself from your family. But ultimately, for my uncle, I think this hadn't really been a choice. He was unable to leave his mother's side.

* * *

One day, I received a call from my parents to tell me that my grandmother had become so frail she had stopped getting out of bed. I took the train up from London. Shortly afterwards, she died at home at the age of ninety-seven – a number she had reached thanks in no small part to Eric's unwavering care. Among her last words to my dad were, 'You'll look after our Eric for me, won't you?' It could be hard to tell which of them was the principal carer.

His mother's death was undoubtedly a huge blow to my uncle, though he didn't really talk about that kind of thing. He had lived with her practically his whole life. We later discovered he'd painted no fewer than five portraits of her. She also appeared in several of his street scenes. Now, at the age of seventy-six, he was on his own for the first time. It wasn't too much to wonder if he would cope. His eccentricities soon began to propagate. The piles of newspapers and magazines started to amass. Though it was hard to tell how much this was behaviour triggered by his mother's departure or, more likely, forces her presence had held back.

Wanting to give him something to look forward to, my dad and my aunt had an idea: they would take their older brother on holiday. In a spirit of gratitude for all that he'd done for their mother, they invited him to join them on a cruise. It was a spirit that would later be tested.

My parents, in retirement, had become seasoned cruisers, my mum having been first inspired to sail by her hairdresser, Pam. Pam lived to cruise, and despite my mum's trepidation that she wasn't a natural seafarer, the ambience of the cruise ship, as powerfully evoked by

Pam, was sufficiently alluring to overcome this. After a one-night mini-cruise to test her sea legs, a flurry of longer cruises followed, including a couple with Pam, and my mum became one of the industry's most enthusiastic evangelists. But the experience wasn't what you'd call a natural fit for my uncle. The very things that appealed to my mum would surely unsettle him: the opulence of the ship, the schedule of events, the fact you lost sight of your luggage from boarding the coach to Southampton until you entered your cabin. Would this offer meet the same reception as the retirement village? But in fact, Eric gratefully accepted. Though not without some trepidation in the weeks leading up to departure.

The proposed trip wasn't the longest of voyages as cruises go, but it was still a significant venture for my uncle. By this time, he walked with a stick, and he had only been on a few, short trips abroad before: the week in Paris, a weekend with my dad in Amsterdam, and a brief trip to Belgium in his youth with a friend who opened beer bottles with his teeth.

What worried him about the cruise was the other passengers. 'They'll all be too posh!' he fretted. I was surprised to learn from my parents that he'd said this. I'd never heard him so openly share this anxiety before. Was this new vulnerability the result of losing his mother and the prospect of such a trip without her? My parents tried to assuage his nerves. The other passengers definitely wouldn't be posh. Though the measure of that is subjective – there certainly wouldn't be anyone opening beer bottles with their teeth. My mum had strategically selected one of the less flashy cruise operators, though again it's all relative. She had to break the news to my uncle that she'd bought him a tuxedo from M&S. For the 'formal dinners' – that very phrase an assault on his nerves. Alongside this, she had bought him a couple of new jumpers, shirts and pairs of trousers. He accepted these, but not the suggestion of a haircut. That was the point at which the whole thing started to feel less like a gift and more like an intervention.

With his walking stick tethered to his wrist, he hobbled aboard the ship in his new attire, a slightly smarter version of his usual self. However, if anyone had imagined his intimidation at mixing with the cruising classes might have a subduing effect on his persona, the opposite proved true. On board, he dialled up his usual schtick, repurposing his nervous energy into a rolling comedy routine aimed at anyone in proximity. It was an act that quickly grew tiring for my parents and my aunt.

My dad explained to me the effort of just walking down a corridor with his brother. He would pitch his stick a few inches ahead of him, then move one foot to catch it up, followed by the other – and repeat. He moved slowly; my dad couldn't begrudge him that. But his inchmeal pace was further reduced by a compulsion to stop and speak to everyone they passed, delivering some small quip.

'I've taken a wrong turn – which way's First Class?'

I've made that one up, but they'd usually be some riff on his own appearance and physical state.

'I'll have a couple at the bar then jog back.'

You get the idea.

His prime territory for this behaviour, my dad recalled,

was the lift. It was impossible for my uncle to observe the unwritten social rule of the lift – smile politely at your fellow travellers then stand in silence. He had to befriend all who entered. And if they seemed averse to that, this only fired him up for the challenge. My dad would stand in the corner smiling apologetically as this played out. Though he had to admit, his brother was surprisingly successful. He noted the startled expressions of people joining them as the lift doors parted to reveal an oddly convivial gathering.

One evening, they went to see an entertainer on the ship, a mind reader whose patter involved ribbing audience members. He quickly homed in on my uncle as rich pickings, asking where he was from. 'You're the bloody mind reader, you tell me,' Eric replied, raising a big laugh. He was certainly skilled at working an audience – the question was how much the audience wished to be worked. Walking down a corridor one day, my dad was sure he saw a couple turn and bolt when they spotted my uncle crawling towards them.

One thing was for sure: any attempt by my parents or my aunt to dissuade him from this behaviour would only have the very opposite effect. Whether they liked it or not, they were along for the ride. The only way out was through.

The greatest test of Eric's nerves was the ship's dining room. On the first night, he was extremely anxious before going in, my mum remembered. At her recommendation, they'd chosen a group table, meaning they would be randomly assigned another four dining companions. These turned out to be a Glaswegian couple in their sixties and, with a slight sense of divine intervention, a mother holidaying with her adult son, Norman. Norman was a tall, large man in his late thirties or early forties. He was single and a qualified nurse. He'd had a tough time in the profession, he said, and was now volunteering at a drug rehabilitation centre. Norman's mother was a plump, white-haired lady in her seventies. She also had another son, she was keen to let everyone know, who was very successful. A lawyer. With a family.

The Glaswegian couple were quiet, middle-class, my mum recalled. They found themselves sitting closest to my uncle, who set about getting to know them – or 'breaking them down', to use his own phrase – by his standard method: an assumed appreciation of working men's club comedy. On the second night, the couple revealed this was the first holiday they'd taken – that they'd felt able to take – since the sudden, tragic death of their son a couple of years earlier. Learning this would do little to alter my uncle's behaviour – a fact known to his family members, who were now feeling slightly concerned about the seating arrangements.

But meanwhile, a more pressing situation was developing. It was becoming increasingly apparent that there was something wrong with Norman. It was my aunt who spotted it first. Norman occasionally seemed a little unresponsive at the dinner table. As the week went on, it became more obvious. His eyelids were heavy. He'd slump slightly while eating. After leaving the dining room one evening, my aunt speculated that perhaps Norman wasn't so much volunteering at the drug rehabilitation centre as attending it.

At first, Norman's mother would make occasional efforts to keep her son in check. 'Norman! Someone's talking to you!' she would snap quietly when her son failed to respond. But as Norman's narcosis grew worse, his mother increasingly dealt with the situation by feigning ignorance. And everyone else, wishing to spare her embarrassment, followed her cue. It was an awkward arrangement that just about held together – until the night of the formal dinner.

The formal evening on a cruise is largely an excuse for people to dress up, the men in dinner suits and the women in evening or cocktail dresses. My mum set the scene for me by explaining that the dining room will offer something a little extra: 'beef Wellington or a Marco Pierre White menu'. For the first time in his life, Eric put on a tuxedo. Norman turned up similarly besuited but it quickly became apparent that he would struggle to fit in with the vibe of the evening. He was unresponsive. His eyelids were drooping. As everyone took their seats, Norman's mother muttered something about him being unwell, but that was as much as she would refer to it. Otherwise, she tried to pretend that everything was normal as, beside her at the table, Norman started slumping forward, his head lopping towards his dinner plate. It was becoming increasingly impossible to ignore – though, for Norman's mother's benefit, everybody did. And then, horror of horrors, a photographer arrived at the table – another tradition of the formal evening – to document the situation.

Most members of the group were keen to have a memento of their time together. Especially the quiet Glaswegian couple, who by now had become firm chums with my uncle. Much less so Norman's mother, though she couldn't bring herself to voice any objection. The photographer directed the men to stand in line behind the seated women, at which point it became clear that Norman couldn't get to his feet. Norman's mother shook her head in quiet mortification. It was difficult to know how to play this. But before anyone had much chance to ponder that, Eric stepped in and, despite his own physical limitations, started helping Norman up: 'I've got you, Norman, kid. You're alright.' The photographer took the picture and the awkward scene was preserved forever: Norman, in a semi-comatose state, being held up by my uncle's tight, arthritic grip, looming over his mother seated in front, her face flushed with shame. The next evening at dinner there were two empty seats at the table. Norman and his mother had decided to dine alone. Or more likely his mother had decided this, unable to bear any further humiliation.

The following day, my parents, my aunt and Eric were eating lunch in a cafeteria on the ship when they spotted Norman and his mother. The pair were sitting alone at a table on the far side of the room. Everyone felt bad about it but the general view was that they should give Norman and his mother some space, and respect their decision to withdraw from the group. Eric, however, disagreed. He picked up his walking stick and got himself to his feet. My parents and aunt tried to dissuade him from whatever it was he was planning, but it was, as ever, useless. He was already bee-lining his way across the cafeteria, slowly but determinedly, towards Norman's and his mother's table.

'Where were you two last night?' he asked as he reached their table.

On the other side of the room, the rest of his group tried to look as inconspicuous as possible, in case Norman's mother mistook them for co-conspirators in this intervention.

'Have you found better company?' my uncle continued. 'And if so, can I join it?'

Allowing herself a smile, Norman's mother admitted she had felt too embarrassed to sit with the group. That she thought it might be better if they dined just the two of them. But Eric wouldn't accept that there was anything to be embarrassed about.

'We've all got our problems,' he told Norman's mother. And then, playing his ace, he added, 'Just look at the state of me.'

They'd been missed, he told the pair – and it strikes me he had extra reason to mean it. It's not difficult to see why my uncle felt an affinity with Norman, a man in an unlikely duo with his mother, with no career or family for her to boast of. Or indeed how Norman was unknowingly supporting my uncle – by being the antithesis of what he feared encountering in the dining room, someone else wrestling demons conjured by the formal evenings.

That evening, Norman and his mother rejoined the table. The awkward atmosphere had lifted. Norman's mother's shame was all but gone. And most curiously of all, from then on, Norman was never anything other than fully conscious at dinner.

Eric's relentless subversion of social etiquette had nearly driven the rest of his party to distraction. But they were amused to concede this was an impressive victory manifested by the very same energy. Somehow, his apparent lack of tact had facilitated a consummate feat of diplomacy.

Here, I think, is the key to understanding my uncle's unorthodox philosophy. Why he was so ardently committed to a lack of airs and graces, to use his own phrase. Formality, decorum, status: these were fictions that got in the way of camaraderie, humanity and the real stuff of life. Even tact and discretion should be treated with suspicion; unnecessary for those with pure intentions, useful to those without. He used humour to disarm people, to defuse their pretences and get more immediately to what lay underneath. From his lack of sophistication, he gained something that he considered more valuable. In life but also, I think, in his art: what fosters greater connection also facilitates greater insight. Polish and refinement might be the stock-in-trade of the art gallery but, for him, they were poison to the artist.

As the trip came to an end, and the group said goodbye to one another, the quiet Glaswegian couple told Eric how much they'd enjoyed his company, how much they'd laughed, and for the first time in a long time. It seemed Eric hadn't just conquered his anxieties, he'd nigh-on conquered the ship. Admittedly, there were some who had fled at the sight of him approaching. And the rest of his party probably felt like they needed a second holiday to recover. But for the most part, Eric's compulsion to share a laugh with everyone – to compère the cruise as if it were the Wheeltappers and Shunters Social Club – had paid off.

Now that I'm familiar with his work, it strikes me that he was trying to create, on the ship, something he was compelled to capture in his paintings: togetherness, belonging, community. The word 'community' has always felt a bit dry and clinical to me. It makes me think of community centres – draughty, characterless halls. But it strikes me that may be because I haven't had a lot of experience of it. And perhaps because, in its best manifestations, it isn't named, it's just felt and experienced; it isn't organised, it just comes about. Which could also make it easy to overlook.

It was an experience in working-class life that my uncle cherished. And what, I think, he felt the rest of his family – and the world in general – had valued too lightly. Status and superiority are inefficacious to its cultivation so, in this at least, the working classes had an advantage. Though I don't think he viewed it as exclusive to them.

He had an unwavering belief that he could make a connection, on his own terms, with anyone and everyone. Introduce him to the monarch and I'm sure he would have behaved the same, with the same reference points and gags – as if he thought we were all, really, if we got over ourselves, working class. He was determined to find that connection even when it seemed elusive. He was certain it was there. Where did his great faith in that come from? Perhaps from the many hours he'd spent looking at and drawing people. Or perhaps it was a belief he had necessarily cultivated as a solitary and yet sociable man. With this approach and these skills, it seems he was always well equipped to survive on his own. But his attachment to his mother was so great that it took her death for him to really find that out. Which he did – at the age of seventy-seven, somewhere in the North Atlantic Ocean.

CHAPTER 8

I'M NOT GOOD ENOUGH YET

Searching through the jumble of stuff Eric left behind after his death, I made a surprising discovery: he had once had an exhibition – of sorts. Among the many browning newspaper clippings in his painting room was a page torn from the *Liverpool Echo*, dated 1963. Folded several times to pocketable size, it almost fell to bits on opening. Crumbling at its creases, with a tear across the middle held together by corroding Sellotape, the article about a 'thirty-one-year-old bachelor' with 'a display of his own paintings in oils' was still just about readable. The display in question wasn't at an art gallery but a pub: the atmospherically named Cemetery Hotel in Warrington, opposite the town's main graveyard – where, a few years before this, my uncle had worked as a gravedigger.

Parts of the article confounded me; they didn't sound like my uncle at all. 'It was a surprise when a head of Christ attracted attention and somebody bought it,' he was quoted as saying. 'Since then, I've reproduced that painting three or four times, and it still sells.' Who on earth was this Christ-painting salesman?! But elsewhere, the picture was all too familiar. My uncle was described as 'a quiet and extremely modest man who finds it difficult to talk about his hobby of painting although he is obviously dedicated to it'. Friends had apparently persuaded him to show his work, the article said. 'I'm not good enough for anyone to talk about me' was his own opinion – a compulsively humble, nigh-on self-sabotaging thing to say before your first exhibition – though I noticed he added the word 'yet'.

My dad and my aunt vaguely remembered the Christ paintings among his earliest efforts, which also included portraits of Elvis and copies of other paintings and photographs. I hadn't known my uncle to be a particular fan of Jesus or Elvis, but I suppose that was the point – he was thinking of what people might want to see, rather than what he wanted to paint. For the local Christian community, there was Jesus; for everyone else, Elvis. It was probably quite a shrewd assessment of the art market in Warrington at the time. And in many ways, it's a reasonable enough approach. But it's one Eric quickly tired of, it seems. He somehow gained a sense that its yields were artistically limited. The *Liverpool Echo* article highlighted one particular painting, not included in the pub exhibition but 'tossed in a corner of the floor' of his studio, that suggested he was beginning, tentatively, to find his own way. It was a self-portrait. My uncle explained how he had just returned home from a day's labouring. He was standing in front of the bathroom mirror, about to shave, when he decided instead to paint himself 'just as you look now' – a working man, dirt, whiskers and all. It seems that once he did turn his focus inward, the paintings became much more difficult to share.

These descriptions of naive early efforts underlined for me just how far my uncle had travelled; how much he had educated himself in art and picture-making. And more than this, how he had started from absolute zero, with parents who were not educated or even particularly interested in art, who didn't take him to galleries, with not even a single art book in the house. He had received no guidance or tuition, no teacher's encouragement. After school, he was apprenticed as a signwriter – that was as close as he got to an art education until my dad took him to a life drawing class when he was in his eighties. He had to figure out, by himself and from scratch, what art was – and what was good art. I wondered how he had found his way on this solitary mission, which artists had influenced him and why. And what had compelled him to keep going for so many years?

Eric rarely spoke to me about art. There were the times, as a child, whiling away school holidays at my grandparents' house, that he gave me a little drawing tuition. His advice generally came down to two things: 'fill the page' and 'know when to stop'. I gave little credence to either, thinking who was *he* to school *me* in my art? On the second point, he would sometimes suddenly urge me to stop – declare my drawing finished, a masterpiece. Other times, he'd look over my shoulder and tell me I'd blown it.

After his death, I realised that I could see these bits of advice, there, in his own work. By 'fill the page' he was exhorting me to make a picture, to create a composition, when instead I was lost in the exhaustive cross-hatching of a small cartoon character. He clearly thought carefully about the design of his work – we found detailed preparatory sketches, sometimes several for one painting, in which he planned his final image. And his paintings, I noticed, never feel overworked. He had a keen sense of when to step away.

I remember my uncle speaking to me about the work of other artists just twice. On one occasion, he gave me an impromptu lecture about why the painting *Mr and Mrs Clark and Percy* was indisputable evidence that David Hockney's talents were greatly overhyped. His argument rested almost entirely on the right-hand thumb of Mr Clark, one of the portrait's two sitters. I was far from convinced as he kept directing me to 'look at that thumb!' while pointing at a picture of the painting in the *Sunday Times Magazine*.

A curious detail here is that Eric had met this thumb's owner, the fashion designer, Ossie Clark. He was my dad's school friend and the two of them had gone to art college together in Manchester. Later, they lost contact as Clark went on to the Royal College of Art and, after that, fashion fame. I wonder if this slight personal connection to the painting gives a clue to Eric's real objection: that he saw it as erasure of working-class culture. A sumptuous portrait of a working-class couple in upmarket surroundings redolent of a lifestyle magazine shoot, the image could be seen as empowering. But perhaps to him it felt more like capitulation. Or perhaps this was a rare expression of bitterness at another artist's success when he hadn't so much as been to art school. Eric, I'm sure, would decry all of that as nonsense and refer me back to the thumb.

I googled the painting recently. Inevitably, I found myself zooming in on the digit in question, amused by the thought of this ridiculous argument, in a way, rolling on thirty years later. Reminding myself it's a brilliant painting, I happened to notice a section of Ossie's seat, between his legs, appears to have been left out. And a portion of the window shutter behind the chair. Stylistic choices, I assumed. But I could already imagine Eric leaping on my questioning of these details as a complete admission of defeat – as he would at the slightest hint of concession to his argument. My sides began to tighten with stirrings of laughter. It was the muscle memory of a hundred such episodes, where losing would somehow turn into who laughed first – the final, unbeatable weapon in his arsenal. But I'm not willing to concede defeat on this one yet. Because sorting through my uncle's sketches, I found studies he'd made of some of Hockney's drawings. He was, I discovered, a secret fan.

On the second occasion he spoke to me about art – and this is characteristic of Eric, whose opinions tended to be based in polar extremes – he showed me a picture of a painting by Edward Burra, impressing on me its virtues and Burra's genius generally. The painting was *Café Bar* from 1930, a richly coloured image of three men in a French bar with strange, jarring perspectives. I had no idea who Edward Burra was but the moment lodged in my memory for my uncle's uncharacteristic earnestness.

Edward Burra became his favourite artist. Born in the sleepy, southern English coastal town of Rye in 1905, Burra is best known for his vibrant watercolours of urban life, though he isn't exactly a household name. During his life, Burra never achieved the status of some of his contemporaries – artists like Paul Nash or Ben Nicholson – and he's had relatively few public exhibitions since his death in 1976. In the art market, however, Burra's work has been quietly appreciating in value. In 2011, his painting *Zoot Suits*, which places four sharp-suited Black men at the centre of a London street scene, sold at auction for more than £2 million.

In Eric's time-capsule bedroom, he had a poster for Burra's 1973 retrospective at the Tate pinned to his wall, which presumably means he went. Certainly, my dad remembered going with him to an exhibition of Burra's work at London's Hayward Gallery in the mid-1980s. As it happens, the gallery's other exhibition at the time, to which most of the visiting crowd was drawn, was 'Hockney Paints the Theatre'. Eric gave it a rather cursory glance, my dad said, before poring over Burra's landscapes: images of snarling lorries lumbering over hillsides, of Britain's changing countryside and the machines and construction projects churning it up, which the writer Rachel Cooke noted are hard to distinguish as 'more a source of regret or delight' for Burra. It's not difficult to see how these images had particular resonance for my uncle, given his line of work. And also why Burra's other themes appealed to him – the surrealist depictions of the horrors of war, which Eric had lived through as a child, and Burra's lively exaltations of street life, nightlife, and low life.

Eric took a keen interest in the lives of artists he admired, as well as their work. Among his books on art were a number of biographies, including Burra's. He felt a kinship with these artists, I think. Perhaps to some extent he sought them out because of this – it bolstered his sense of himself, and his own validity as an artist, in a world that provided him with little of either.

That said, the similarities between Eric Tucker and Edward Burra aren't obvious. Like many well-known artists, Burra came from a wealthy family. He was privately educated and had a relatively long formal training in art. But he was also something of an outsider, a loner, who never quite fit into any art scene or movement. 'Always join the minority,' he said, echoing Eric's own sentiment that, whichever way momentum was travelling, he was usually 'headed the other road'.

There was one thing they had in common. Burra fought a painful, lifelong battle with rheumatoid arthritis. It's thought to be the reason he favoured watercolour, a lighter medium that allowed him to work more comfortably on a tabletop. Eric also suffered with severe arthritis, though not since childhood like Burra. He had developed a condition called spondylitis in middle age: a painful, chronic inflammation of the spine and other joints, the result of his years of physical labour. I remember he found it difficult to hold a pen – a fact which made the discovery that he'd produced hundreds of drawings and paintings during this time seem all the more unbelievable.

To be clear, I don't believe this was Eric's main attraction to Burra. I think he responded deeply to the artist's work regardless of this fact. But it's fortuitous that Burra's retrospective at the Tate arrived shortly before arthritis became a very real issue for my uncle, seriously threatening his artistic practice.

Inspired by Burra, he began increasingly painting in watercolour, though it seems he also determinedly kept working in his beloved oils. His watercolour paintings cover all his usual subjects – the street, the bar, the circus – but they also open up another area of interest in landscape and the natural world. Many of them are paintings of West Pembrokeshire where we took our family holidays. It's like he quietly made the area his own Provence. In fact, I was struck by how his many studies of Carn Llidi, a hill right at the edge of the Welsh peninsula, seem to echo Cézanne's paintings of Mont Sainte-Victoire; his own modest version of the master's motif.

'When did he do them all?!' my mum said, incredulous, as we looked through these paintings. Numerous aspects of my uncle's story seem to defy the laws of physics. How, for example, paintings that now filled two sizeable storage rooms had been largely hidden around his modest house. But these paintings were perhaps the most perplexing because we had been with him on holiday and noticed no art-making. It seems he made detailed drawings of locations, in quiet moments alone, which he took back home with him to work up into paintings.

Some of these locations I recognised. And so, on a recent visit to the area, I decided to go looking for them. One was a street scene, a row of cottages stepping down a hill in the tiny city of St Davids, peopled with the ghostly, anachronistic characters my uncle seemed to see everywhere. It's painted on a piece of cardboard, roughly torn at the edges. I'd guess he sketched the outline in situ before squirrelling it into his suitcase for colour to be added back at home. Studying the image on my phone screen, I tried to locate his vantage point, which led me to climb and stand on top of an old, stone garden wall about four and a half feet high. Passers-by were giving me funny looks. I half expected the wall's owner to come out of their house and rightly have a go. Was it really possible that my uncle had drawn this picture so conspicuously?

Another watercolour – one of my favourites of his Pembrokeshire paintings – took me to the little inlet of Porthclais Harbour. In the mid-afternoon sun, I trudged along the dusty coastal path on the cliff overlooking the harbour, heading towards the open sea. A few sparkling boats bobbed below me on the calm, green water behind the jetty, their hulls gently knocking. In search of the painting's viewpoint, which looks into the harbour from outside of the jetty, I left the path and started scrambling down the grassy bank towards the water. Outside the harbour's shelter, there was a sharp breeze. Waves crashed against the sheer rock faces beneath me. I was edging precariously towards the surf, but I still hadn't reached the angle of the painting. My foot slipped a little on shingle stones and I decided to call it a day. I knew enough. My uncle, with spondylitis, appeared to have scrambled down to the rocks in order to get the view he wanted – an impressive dedication for a painting that nobody would see during his lifetime.

My dad spoke to his brother about art more often. Generally, it led to an argument. His interest was almost exclusively in figurative painting, my dad said, though within that his tastes could be unexpected. But he had no time whatsoever for abstract expressionism, the de rigueur movement of his day. My dad would try to challenge his brother's firm opinions – what he saw as his rather narrow, obsessive focus. As the one who'd been to art school, he dared to imagine he could educate his brother. On reflection, he told me, he had failed to appreciate how much time his brother had spent thinking about these things. Though occasionally he was sharply reminded.

He recalled an instance during their cruise holiday. They had stopped at the port of Bilbao and were visiting the Guggenheim Museum. Hobbling around the gallery with his stick, Eric was decidedly unimpressed by most of the work on display. He and my dad were bickering about it. Tempers were rising. Then Eric launched into a critique of one particular painting with such eloquence and conviction that he managed to silence my dad, who then noticed members of a passing tour group peeling off to listen. The tour guide looked irked as, one by one, and then with unstoppable momentum, he lost his entire group.

My dad believed his brother had received his art education, for the largest part, from regular visits to Manchester's two public galleries. Even into his seventies and early eighties, with his mobility failing, he would catch a bus to the city to get a pint and visit a gallery. My dad marvelled at his determination. The journey was nearly two hours each way, weaving through the orbital towns of Irlam, Eccles and Salford. It was a pilgrimage he'd been making for decades, but how had he first found his way into these galleries? My dad wasn't sure, except that he started visiting the city in his teens. Presumably, it was his interest in art that led him inside, so where, then, had this first been kindled? Where had he first been exposed to art?

It seems unlikely that his brief schooling had made any meaningful impression in this area. And growing up, none of Eric's immediate family had any great interest in art. But in the wider family, there was one intriguing exception to this, I discovered. One of my grandmother's cousins was a man named Tom Malone. Tom was an 'Inspector of Weights and Measures' for Salford Council but also, in his spare time, chairman of the local art club. An accomplished portraitist, he painted a number of local dignitaries, alongside landscapes and still lifes. He had even known L.S. Lowry. (As an aside, I note that's now two monolithically famous painters – Lowry and Hockney – who, you could say, my uncle was one handshake away from. The sentiment is a bit of a stretch with Hockney – my dad had known Ossie Clark in his youth – but it still feels remarkable enough for a man who, by any reasonable measure, was about as far outside the art world as can be. It's not a thought that ever occurred to my uncle, I'm sure. And it's a quirk more than a contradiction in the story, I think – evidence perhaps of how near and yet far we are from one another.) I asked my dad about his mother's cousin, Tom. He had heard her mention him but he had no memory of ever meeting the man, nor of his older brother ever speaking about him. So was this just a curious coincidence? Evidence of a creative gene in my grandmother's family? Or had my uncle been in some way inspired by his mother's cousin? Perhaps even just through knowledge of his existence. If so, he never talked about it. But then he never talked about a lot of things.

My dad believed his brother's first impressions of art came from the magazines that he voraciously collected. An early manifestation of his hoarding instinct, it makes sense to me as a precursor to his art-making: the urge to collect and preserve. Some of my dad's earliest memories are of sharing a room with his older brother: the second, small bedroom of a two-up two-down – the first house they lived in – which, alongside the two brothers, also had to accommodate my uncle's various collections. My dad distantly recalled a chest of drawers full of birds' eggs, carefully blown and neatly compartmentalised. Then later, a wardrobe piled high – higher than my dad – with magazines, until they eventually displaced any room for clothing entirely. At first, these magazines were all boxing-related, then increasingly, over time, magazines on culture. There were articles in them on artists and exhibitions that caught my uncle's eye.

Later, at the end of the 1950s, when Eric had started to pursue painting, the family got a television. It opened up another small cultural window to him, through programmes on art that he sought out in the schedule. Specifically, my dad remembered watching a documentary with his brother on L.S. Lowry. At the time, Lowry was starting to find widespread fame, though he was still considered something of a provincial oddity whose appraisal by critics didn't match his popular appeal.

I found the film on YouTube and watched it, trying to discern what effect it might have had on my uncle some sixty years ago. It shows the grand, austere stone house where Lowry lived and worked in Mottram in Longdendale, a village whose other famous residents have included the serial killer Dr Harold Shipman and the lady who played Nora Batty – the full scope of northern heroes and villains.

Lowry is shown painting in a three-piece suit, complete with a handkerchief in the breast pocket of his paint-spattered jacket. The dour décor of his house is brightened slightly by collections of ornate clocks and Rosetti drawings, though both these things add to the sense that we're not in the 1950s but the 1880s.

I was immediately struck by how very different Lowry appears to my uncle: formal and remote; dressed like a provincial bank clerk, or perhaps the manager of an isolated train station. That said, in his own way, Eric had a similar sense of being trapped in a bygone era, of being born out of time. Perhaps this was the result of a shared biographical detail: Lowry was also a lifelong bachelor who lived with his mother until her death. When my uncle watched this film, these facts were only just beginning to establish themselves in his life. But perhaps what lay behind them caused my uncle to feel an affinity with the eccentric painter. I noticed Lowry describe himself as 'a very lonely sort of person'.

I could imagine Eric enjoying the way Lowry speaks in the film. His aloof, matter-of-fact vernacular, refusing to philosophise on what he paints and why. To artists who complain of their work not selling – an experience Lowry had been familiar with – he's wryly unsympathetic: 'Why should you expect people to buy your pictures?' he barks. 'They haven't asked you to paint them.'

He seems to offer an uncompromising but simple philosophy for artists, one that's easy to imagine Eric having taken to heart: that you need justify yourself to no one, and no one is who you should expect the patronage of.

It struck me that it may have been interesting to my uncle that Lowry, despite his formal training, consciously painted in a naive style. It's a strange paradox to first encounter, like a classically trained pianist choosing to play 'Chopsticks'. It was part of what liberated my uncle, possibly, to move beyond the painterly realism he sought to achieve – and largely did – in earlier work. Most of all, my dad believed his brother was inspired by Lowry to 'paint from where he stood'. Lowry allowed him to see that, though the art world might be a remote, exclusive domain, art itself was not, and the world he inhabited was worthy subject matter for it. Perhaps here, Eric also felt that the painter had missed something about the experience of working-class life. He was certainly a fan of Lowry, but it might be easy to overstate his influence on my uncle's work, given the subject matter, above that of others. I noticed, for example, that among his art books, he had just one on Lowry.

Eric's book collection, which he kept in his painting room, piled up on a couple of insubstantial bookcases, was an eclectic mix to behold. Aside from the art books, there were biographies of boxers, left-wing political figures, gangsters, music hall performers, comedians and clowns. There were horse-racing annuals, woefully outdated road maps and novels both highbrow and low, from Henry Miller to Ian Fleming. A book on the nineteenth-century landscape painter John Constable sat incongruously next to *Hard Bastards*, a compendium of Britain's toughest men.

His art books tended to be second-hand or of the cheap, slim, schoolboyish variety. They seem unlikely to represent a comprehensive list of the art he saw and admired, but still a good indication. Now packed away in boxes, I searched through them, taking stock of the periods and artists they covered. As I picked them up, blank and half-filled betting slips rained out from between the pages, marking sections of particular interest. I noticed a distinctly British vein among the titles, from Walter Sickert to Lucian Freud. But for the very largest part, they were books on early Modern artists, mostly Post-Impressionists: Cézanne, Degas, Toulouse-Lautrec, Gauguin, Van Gogh and Chagall. He was interested in these artists' lives as well as their work, my dad thought. 'He liked their rebellious character – the fact they didn't walk away from low life, they were absorbed by it and absorbed into it.' Van Gogh had been an early favourite, my dad recalled – the key to opening up this period to him. Again, he'd been as interested in Van Gogh's life as his art, owning a well-thumbed copy of the artist's letters.

It makes sense to me that Eric's understanding of art was rooted in this period and these artists. That, from them, he'd formulated ideas of where to look and what to paint in his own world. At first, perhaps, a simple sense of what seemed certifiably artistic. But through practice, and looking, he found something more personal and deeply felt, the subjects and themes that became his obsessions. Most of his work can be organised into three distinct categories: street scenes, bar and pub scenes, and images of the circus and theatreland. In all, he emphasises the characterful richness of so-called ordinary life, and elevates the lowly and the marginal. Even his images of showbusiness revel in its tawdry glamour, celebrating not its stars but its itinerant journeyman performers. He returned to these themes again and again, and within them, though the vast majority of his work is undated, it's possible to chart the development. His characters become less naturalistic but I think, for him, more real. Later, they grow increasingly ethereal, more like memories of people, as if he's painting his world disappearing. Throughout, he maintains an uncommon mix of sophistication and innocence: a perfect reflection of his character and his idiosyncratic self-education in art.

As I've become more familiar with his paintings, carrying them around in my head, I'll sometimes feel I spot a reference to another artist's work – when I'm visiting an exhibition, say. Sometimes it's obvious. His painting *Card Players*, for example, is clearly his own version, transposed to a northern pub, of the same subject painted by Cézanne, Caillebotte and others before them. Other times I can only wonder. A number of his paintings contain a picture within the picture – is this a reference to the work of Vermeer? Is the proliferation of carefully arranged bottles in his bar scenes a nod to the Italian still-life painter Giorgio Morandi? Perhaps, perhaps not. I can't know for sure. But I won't underestimate a man who, with failing legs, takes a two-hour bus ride to a gallery.

Among Eric's paintings, there was a small portrait of a man in profile. My dad recognised him. 'That was Keith,' he said. Keith lived around the corner from my uncle and, like him, had never left home. Eric knew him to say hello to. Keith had no idea, of course, that his portrait had been painted. 'Keith's life was just work, the pub, the bookie's,' my dad said, cheerfully. My uncle will have sincerely admired that about him. He was just the sort of apparently inconsequential figure that Eric found to be anything but. And my dad's description of Keith could almost have fitted my uncle – but for the glaring exception of a house stuffed full of artwork.

Eric was an intelligent, curious and creative man, given no real opportunity to develop these qualities through formal education. His circumstances didn't exactly bring art to him – in fact, he grew up in surroundings almost bereft of it – but it reached him anyway, through his hunger to seek it out. His antenna picked up the signals, however faint at first. He voraciously consumed the morsels and they began to form a trail. His early, insatiable impulse to collect seemed to have no reason. But then a reason began to emerge – it met with his burgeoning enthusiasm for first drawing and then painting, through the articles he read on art and the photographs he saved as references. It all became a part of what fed into his creative practice.

He hadn't been afforded the opportunity to go to art school, so he had to find his own way. But in many ways, this suited his nature: the complete liberty to chart his own course and follow his nose. And with no sense that he was part of the art world, even in the smallest, most peripheral way, he wasn't unduly influenced by the contemporary. He was, you could say, freer to float around art history, landing on the work he responded to the most and making the work truest to himself.

In the age of the internet, this kind of self-learning is easier than ever – images and tutorials are there at a click. But in a time before this, Eric's journey was inchmeal. From a standing start, he made each discovery alone, by doing the work and by looking at work, which generally required some effort to seek out. But his determination to keep going was unwavering. Making art was necessary for him, though sharing it was not.

He didn't have the encouragement of a tutor or the fellowship of a group, but he found these things in the lives of the artists whose work spoke to him. His life provided him with little opportunity to express this most significant part of himself, but he made sense of it and nourished it, I think, through the kinship he felt with them. Burra, Lowry, Van Gogh – they were each, in their own way, outsiders, not a part of any clique or group. They were also loners. Like my uncle, Burra and Lowry were interminably single. Van Gogh was not what you'd call lucky in love. Each conjured beauty out of – or in spite of – adversity. Burra's arthritis forced him to work in watercolour – and his achievements in the medium are unparalleled. Van Gogh created masterpieces in spite of serious mental ill health. Financial troubles forced Lowry's family to downgrade from their middle-class, leafy suburb to industrial Pendlebury – and the rest is history. Their work, their characters, and their life stories sustained and vitalised my uncle on his solitary journey.

That journey began in earnest, I discovered, with an explosion of creative energy, not long before the *Liverpool Echo* visited Eric on the eve of his pub exhibition. In a familiar scene, in his painting room there were 'finished and unfinished paintings everywhere,' the article said, 'on a chest of drawers, on the floor, on the walls, under chairs'. Noting his other interest in boxing, my uncle admitted that 'since this painting bug got really into my bloodstream, I've got no time for sport'. The bug would stay with him for the rest of his life. But it would be fifty-five years before he raised the prospect of another exhibition. Perhaps that was how long it took for him to feel that, now, finally, he was good enough for somebody to talk about.

CHAPTER 9

THE FINAL (SORT OF) WISH

Aged eighty-four, Eric was diagnosed with a degenerative heart condition. Essentially, his heart was slowly failing. A consultant at the local hospital explained to him that there was no cure, but treatments were available: medication and the fitting of a pacemaker, which together would improve his symptoms and extend his life. Without them, the condition was sure to worsen and he wouldn't have long to live. He reported this back to my dad – along with the fact that he'd decided not to bother with the pacemaker. Naturally, my dad tried to persuade him to reconsider, but it was the retirement village all over again. Though this time with life-or-death stakes.

My dad went along with Eric to a follow-up appointment at the hospital. Perhaps a doctor would be more successful at changing his brother's mind. My dad explained that his brother had some reservations about the pacemaker and the consultant did his best to reassure my uncle – the operation was a simple one, he would be out of hospital the same day, and the treatment was effective. But my uncle was unmoved.

Something of a campaign began in the family, with all of us trying to persuade Eric to have the operation. His reasoning against it seemed maddeningly irrational and defeatist. It would only be postponing the inevitable. It wasn't worth the trouble. We tried to make him see sense.

THE FINAL (SORT OF) WISH

The operation was a common procedure – and free! And 'postponing the inevitable' meant potentially years of extra life! Not to mention the fact his symptoms would be alleviated. But deploying these kinds of logical arguments only caused him to become further entrenched in his position. He had made up his mind.

It was against this backdrop, with his mortality in sharp focus, that Eric mentioned, one day when my dad was visiting, how he would have liked to have had an exhibition at the local museum and gallery. So began the cataloguing, and the unfolding discovery of just how much work Eric had produced. My dad would contact the local museum, he said, and see if he could get someone to take a look at his brother's work. This was the kind of suggestion that usually spooked my uncle. The offer would be waved off or met with a stone wall of indifference. But now, he seemed more open to it. If he did have an exhibition, Eric piped up, he would dedicate it to his late father. It appeared he had given this some thought.

I remember learning about these developments from my mum, over the phone. It felt intriguing and a little exciting, like perhaps my uncle's main obstacle – himself – had finally gotten out of his way. But I also knew not to get involved. That was by invitation only. One wrong move and it was only too easy to imagine him swiftly reverting to type and closing back down.

My dad's visits to his brother's house were now consumed with cataloguing: working his way through another stack of paintings, making another dent in the emerging pile. The vast majority were untitled, so together, for purposes of cataloguing, he and his brother named them – often inspired by some particular detail of the scene. Progress was slow at first, as each painting brought back memories of a venue long closed or a view since changed, but eventually, they began to find a rhythm. Some titles required careful thought. Others were decidedly easier. My dad carried through an oil painting of cloth-capped men in a bar adorned with titillating pictures, including one of a lady bending over. 'Bare Arsed', my uncle offered up at a glance, from his chair. My dad scribbled all this down in his ledger book. Categories and subcategories were created as they went. Numbering systems were revised on the hoof, letters added. Works were crossed out and moved to another page or section. These sessions would go on until Eric grew too tired or my dad could no longer carry paintings.

Meanwhile, my dad made contact with the local museum. He called the number for general enquiries and asked if he could speak to whoever organised their art exhibitions. He explained that his elderly brother was a self-taught painter, a retired labourer from the town who had produced a significant body of work which had never before been exhibited.

It isn't easy for an artist to get a solo exhibition at a public museum or gallery. If they're lucky, it might happen decades into an established career, longer even. And I suspect arrangements don't often begin with their representative calling the number for general enquiries. But my dad hoped that if he could just persuade someone to come and look at his brother's work, they might see the value in it.

THE FINAL (SORT OF) WISH

Unfortunately, the exhibitions officer wasn't available to come to the phone right now, my dad was told. So a week later, he tried again. But again the exhibitions officer wasn't available. Nor again when he tried for a third time.

While this was going on, the cataloguing continued. As the scale of the task grew, my dad enlisted the help of my mum – an act of delegation more than Eric could bear. 'No, no, no!' he cried when he saw the new recruit. He insisted my mum must not touch any of the paintings, but my dad managed to persuade him that her help was needed. She returned a pair of catalogued works back to the bedroom where they had been stashed, while my dad fetched two more.

'You're putting them back wrong!' my uncle shouted up from his chair downstairs.

'You don't know how I'm putting them back, Eric, you can't see me!' my mum shouted back.

'No,' he replied, 'but I can hear.'

My dad decided to step up his campaign with the museum. After failing to get through on the phone, he went there in person, armed with some photographs of his brother's work. He approached a junior member of staff and asked if he could see the exhibitions officer. The staff member scuttled off to find out, returning moments later with the message that, unfortunately, the exhibitions officer was in a meeting.

A week or so later my dad returned. This time he took some of Eric's actual paintings with him – no small feat to get his brother to agree to. Again, my dad approached a member of staff and, again, the message came back that the exhibitions officer was in a meeting. My dad asked if there was anyone else he could speak to. Everyone was in a meeting, he was told. However, perhaps by now recognising that he wasn't going to stop, the staff member agreed to pass on my dad's contact details. It was a sliver of progress.

By now, the effects of my uncle's heart condition, along with his worsening arthritis, were making it increasingly difficult for him to continue living at home. But he refused to consider any alternative. He struggled to get upstairs – he'd had a Stannah stairlift installed some years earlier, but even reaching this had become difficult – so he asked my dad to bring down his bed. He would live and sleep in the back living room. My dad knew that any discussion about the viability of this was pointless, so the following Saturday he and my brother came over to move the bed.

They took the mattress off and began by transporting the bed frame. It was, at least, a single bed but the task was still an awkward one. My uncle's bedroom was full of stuff. The back room downstairs was full of even more stuff. There were two doorways to pass through, low ceilings, and a narrow staircase, with several turns and rickety bannisters, to navigate. My dad and my brother had to twist and turn the bed, lever it from horizontal to vertical and back again, as they manoeuvred it towards its destination. Eric, meanwhile, had positioned himself at the bottom of the stairs, resting on his Zimmer frame. From here, he issued continual instructions and a running commentary on my dad's lack of competence at the task. 'Tony, Tony, Tony – what are you doing? Anyone can see you don't want to do it like that!' In return, my dad, whose fuse isn't the longest when not hauling a bed frame, directed a rising crescendo of profanities at his older brother. Eventually, they made it downstairs to the back room, only to have to return for the mattress and run the gauntlet again.

Eric's new set-up, with his bed in the back living room, was a sight to behold. His hoarded magazines and newspapers were still piled up on the sofa and other surfaces. There was no great tidy-up to make way for the bed – he wouldn't permit it – so everything was pushed to the sides. Though one day while visiting, my aunt had attempted to stuff as much as she could into a bin bag when Eric wasn't looking. There was a narrow walkway around the bed and to his chair in the corner, where he'd laid a plank of wood across the arms as a makeshift table. On the walls, he had hung portraits he'd painted of departed family members: his father, his mother, and his grandmother. It gave the eerie impression that he was preparing to see them again. Among the jumble, and though he was barely mobile, I noticed his easel and oil paints had made their way into the room. Astonishingly, it seemed he was still painting – something I'd thought he probably hadn't been able to do for years or even longer.

Though Eric was deteriorating, my dad hadn't given up on persuading him to get a pacemaker. In fact, he thought his brother's worsening symptoms might have loosened him up to the idea. He went with him to another hospital appointment. This time they saw a different consultant. Again, my dad looked to the doctor to back up his case. The consultant went over the potential benefits of the operation, though more lukewarmly than his predecessor, my dad thought. In the end, it was my uncle's case he backed up. If Eric didn't want to go through with the operation, he told my dad, then that was his choice. It was the end of the line for the pacemaker argument. My uncle's fate was set.

The telephone rang at my parents' house. My mum answered it. It was the exhibitions officer at the local museum. By bad luck, he had called when my dad was out. My mum tried to give a brief overview of why my dad had wanted to speak to him. She asked if my dad could call him back. The exhibitions officer suggested instead sending him an email.

Email is not my dad's natural medium. At work, he had ignored them completely, part of a series of tactics to speed up his early retirement. But also because he couldn't really use a computer. In more recent years, I'd set him up with his own email address. But if you sent something to it, you had to also let him know by other means.

Nevertheless, that evening he parked himself at my mum's laptop and began to compose a message to the exhibitions officer. Subject: 'Eric Tucker, local painter'.

It took a while to write. A latecomer to the technology, he typed slowly, with no muscle memory for the keyboard layout, his index finger searching for each key. One letter at a time, he told the exhibitions officer about his brother. How he had painted all his life, how he had worked as a labourer and educated himself in art, how there were hundreds of paintings in his house. He explained that his brother would like an exhibition and that he'd been attempting to catalogue all the paintings. 'But my ill health (and his) has slowed the process,' he wrote. Without saying it directly, my dad made it pretty clear that his brother was short on time: 'At the age of eighty-six he suffers from a longstanding arthritic condition and heart failure.' In matters like this, you have to deploy all weapons in your arsenal and that includes emotional blackmail. He invited the exhibitions officer to Eric's house – to meet the artist and see his work in person. In the meantime, he would send through some pictures, he said. He signed off the email and clicked 'send'. And then, because my dad doesn't know how to attach images to an email, he followed up with nine consecutive emails sent from my mum's iPad, each containing a full-resolution photograph of a painting. If nothing else, the exhibitions officer would struggle to miss this in his inbox.

A week later, my dad received a response. The exhibitions officer explained that the next few weeks were very busy at the museum and it may take him a while to consider the proposal and respond.

By now, it was becoming clear that Eric didn't have much time left. Family, friends, and neighbours did what they could – what he'd allow – to help him. For a while already, my mum had been doing his laundry. She would deliver his clean clothes in a Bag for Life, which she was instructed to leave just inside his front door. From here, it was unclear how or even if they made it to any drawers or wardrobe. My brother's wife delivered his groceries, and Eric's friend Mr Hassan placed his bets and supplied him with Mrs Hassan's homemade dals and curries. My aunt and her husband, my uncle Frank, tried to make his set-up in the back room more comfortable. They replaced his old bed frame with an orthopaedic one. As Eric was now largely bedridden, it occurred to them to ask him how he turned off the main light before bed. He didn't, he said. It was on all night, making it difficult for him to sleep. So Frank rigged up a cord switch over his bed for him to pull. Then later, when they realised Eric could no longer lift his arm to reach it, Frank extended the cord, tying it to his bed frame so that he only had to knock it with his hand. Arriving one day to find five- and ten-pound notes scattered across the blanket, Frank made a small bedside table for him to keep his money in. Eventually, there was an almost Wallace-and-Gromit-like inventiveness to the contraptions surrounding my uncle, facilitating his existence. But as fast as one problem was solved, several more presented themselves.

Throughout this period, there was a series of medical emergencies, usually a fall. Eric's legs would lose power as his weakening heart struggled to pump blood around his body. His joints stiff with arthritis, he then couldn't get back up. On one occasion, he spent an entire night lying on the carpet until someone found him in the morning. But he still wouldn't consider a care home. Ambulances were increasingly called to his house, though never by him. Sometimes after assessing him, the paramedics would decide he could remain at home – his firm wish. Other times, they took him to the hospital, where he would immediately start plotting how to get out. He was extremely worried about being away from his paintings.

THE FINAL (SORT OF) WISH

On top of this, his mistrust of all but a dwindling minority of people had reached new heights. For the avoidance of doubt, this wasn't dementia – if anything, it was more like a sharpening of long-held inclinations. Family members weren't exempt from suspicion. Especially those, like my mum, who tried to bring him to meet with reality and wouldn't just facilitate his whims.

On his first stay in hospital, he learned that my mum had been visiting his house – to check on it, collect his post, and tidy up a little. This greatly concerned him. He asked my brother to go there and take photographs of his paintings, to show to him. What exactly he thought might be happening to them, I don't know. I'm pretty sure he didn't either. My brother agreed to do it – the time for arguing had passed. Then, as soon as he left the hospital, he called our mum and asked her, since she was going to the house anyway, to take photographs of the paintings to prove she wasn't messing with them. Which, irritated, she did.

On Eric's second admission to hospital, my mum was his principal visitor, because my dad was ill himself with a chest infection. It was a situation suboptimal to my uncle, but he had more pressing concerns. On admission, he'd been diagnosed with flu. He considered this something of a conspiracy to detain him since he didn't feel – or, in fact, look – like he had the flu. When my mum arrived to see him, he informed her that he wanted to get out. She would ask the nurse when they thought he'd be discharged, she said.

'No, you don't understand,' my uncle replied, 'I want to go *now*.'

'Literally now?' my mum asked.

'Yes.'

My mum went to find the nurse in charge of the ward. She explained that her brother-in-law wished to leave the hospital immediately. The nurse told her this wasn't advisable. My mum replied that she understood it wasn't advisable but, nevertheless, he wanted to go. The nurse nodded. Eric would need to leave with his medication, she said, and the doctor wasn't expected to visit the ward for another three or four hours, so he would need to wait until at least then. My mum reported this back to my uncle.

'Bugger the medication! I'm leaving now!'

My mum wasn't getting the message here: my uncle wasn't seeking permission, he was looking for an accomplice. Ever the rule-follower, my mum returned to the nurse to explain that her brother-in-law didn't care about his medication, he just wanted to leave immediately. The nurse nodded. He would need an ambulance to take him home, she said, which probably wouldn't be available until the following morning. This was the final straw for my uncle.

'Get our Ralph on the phone!' (That's my brother who, thanks to his good work with the photographs, was now my uncle's go-to fixer.) 'Tell him to book me a disabled taxi!'

After some ringing around, to the backdrop of Eric urging haste, my mum managed to reach my brother. The disabled taxi was booked and Eric made his escape, sans medication. In fact, my aunt later discovered, he had masses of medication for his heart condition at home – because it appeared he wasn't taking it, perhaps was even hiding it. She found boxes of it 'all over the place', she told me, even in the washing machine.

It's fair to say that these final months of my uncle's life didn't bring out the best in him, as they probably don't in many people. But he had a particularly visceral need for autonomy and independence: the very things his failing health and mobility were stealing from him.

Once he was back home, installed again in his bed, the cataloguing continued. My dad hadn't heard back from the museum's exhibitions officer. Nearly two months had passed since he'd emailed, and the prospect of an exhibition – certainly of one anytime soon – was looking very slim. But cataloguing the work gave my dad something constructive to do with his brother, who was now fading fast, during what were increasingly painful visits. Soon my uncle grew too weak to participate and, with a nod and a wave of his hand, he instructed my dad to carry on the task without him.

Not long after this, when my dad and aunt were with him at his house, a visiting carer informed them that she thought my uncle had suffered a haemorrhage. She called for an ambulance. Despite my uncle's protests, he was taken to hospital. As soon as they arrived at A&E, my aunt remembered, though her brother hardly had strength to move, he turned to her and said, 'Karen, you'll get me out of here, won't you?' She told him that she was working on it. But this time, it wasn't to be.

I got the call that my uncle was dying and caught a train up from London to see him one last time. Although it hardly seemed like him. Lying unconscious in a small room in the hospital, with the sun streaming in between the blinds and the faint whiff of disinfectant in the air, he was still and silent apart from the sound of his uneven breath. His complexion was pale and his cheeks sunken. My parents and my aunt went to get a coffee, leaving me alone with him. They say that hearing is the last sense to go, so I spoke to my uncle as I sat with him. For the first time in my life, I told him that I loved him – words that, to be spoken aloud between us, required one party to be unconscious. I told him he had been more like a second father to me than an uncle. Remembering my brother's story of their car journey to Pembrokeshire, when Eric had spoken of his regret of never having children, I wanted him to know that was only technically true. And I promised him that we would get his paintings seen; a foolish promise, really, because I had absolutely no idea how. I returned to London and, that night, Eric died of heart failure at the age of eighty-six.

When I first learned of my uncle's wish for an exhibition, and the fact he was allowing my dad to sort through his paintings, it was the first time I really thought about how many there might be in his house. I felt like I'd never seen more than a dozen or so, lined up in rows in his painting room. Perhaps there could be thirty, I thought. Then again, he'd been at it a while. Though it was hard to gauge how frequently, and for how long he'd been able to continue given his arthritis. Maybe there could be as many as eighty paintings, I dared to imagine, arbitrarily landing on a number that felt ambitious but not totally impossible. By the time of my uncle's death, my dad had found more than two hundred paintings in his house. In fact, he had uncovered less than half of his work. In the weeks following his death, as my parents tried to bring his house into some sort of order, they would ring me each day to tell me they'd found another thirty, forty, fifty paintings, stashed away in every nook and corner of the house, inside and out. The eventual number, which we were only able to establish when cataloguing was completed two years later, was five hundred and forty. On top of this, there were drawings and sketches too copious to count. His house was bursting at the seams with artwork.

It seemed unbelievable, but in another way, it made perfect sense – a little like discovering a vast escape tunnel dug by a prisoner with just a spoon. Behind a half-closed door, my uncle had doggedly worked away, drawing little to no attention to it, certainly never discussing it, just quietly doing the work. When and how much, we never really knew. The clues were there, but nobody was really looking.

I felt a strange mixture of grief and elation. My uncle was gone but we had also just discovered a vast body of work that completely embodied his character and his life. It felt almost as if he hadn't gone at all but had transmogrified into a hoard of paintings. At the same time, I also had a feeling that I had only just come to really know him.

Seeing all this work for the first time, I was moved to realise that my uncle was an artist. Of course, to some extent I'd known that. But what I'd thought of as maybe a pastime – inasmuch as I thought about it at all – I realised was the centre of his life, at the core of who he was. In an instant, my perception of him shifted. Even his various eccentricities seemed to make a new kind of sense, rearranging themselves around this fact. His uncompromising nature, his need for control, his obsessive collecting, even his lifelong attachment to his mother: they were all practically clichés of an artist's life. If nothing else, I thought, nobody could deny that he really meant it. He had earned his exhibition. But how – or indeed if – he would get it, I had no idea.

This was the start of learning many things about my uncle that I hadn't known. Sometimes this could be an unsettling, or even a slightly painful, experience. Particularly when the new information came from someone I hardly knew.

A little while after my uncle's death, his friend from the bookmaker's, Mr Hassan, told me a story. After discovering he was an artist, Mr Hassan had asked my uncle to paint his portrait, he told me, laughing a little at the memory.

'I only wish I could, but my hands won't let me,' Eric had replied.

My uncle had told his friend all about his heart condition, it transpired. Mr Hassan knew that he needed a pacemaker – and that he was refusing to get one. Like us, Mr Hassan had also been petitioning Eric to go ahead with the operation. Like us, he'd had no success. But he had gotten more of an explanation. And like the discovery of his paintings, it was a surprise to me – and yet, with hindsight, rather obvious.

THE FINAL (SORT OF) WISH

'I said to him, "Why don't you get it done? So that your heart is better."'

My uncle had then raised both his hands, Mr Hassan said.

'But these will still be the same,' he'd answered.

CHAPTER 10

THE DREAMS OF YOUTH

Following my uncle's death, I received an intriguing email. It was from a man called Brian Thompson. He had worked with my uncle, he explained, one summer in the early 1960s, in the delivery yard of the building company where my uncle spent most of his working life. Though they worked together for just a few weeks, 'he left a lasting impression on me,' Brian wrote. But the line that caught my attention: 'His ambition was to go to St Ives and be a painter.'

I'd never heard Eric say this or anything like it. In fact, I'd never heard him voice any kind of personal aspiration at all. I'd viewed his late-life opening up around his artwork and the idea of an exhibition as a lowering of the guard; a change of policy, prompted by time running out. But Brian's email made me reassess that. Perhaps it was more like the last flicker of a dream long since dimmed but never completely extinguished.

I gave Brian a call.

A retired architectural model maker, originally from Warrington, Brian now lived near Preston. Eighty-two years old, I would've sworn from speaking to him that he was twenty years younger. I interrupted him digging up roots in his garden – a welcome interruption, he assured me – for a brief but illuminating conversation.

A friend of Brian's had told him about the pensioner

from Warrington who had died recently, leaving behind hundreds of paintings in his modest terraced house. Brian immediately suspected that the pensioner in question was my uncle, the man he'd worked with sixty years earlier. Though they'd only spent a few short weeks together, and though Brian had never even seen any of Eric's paintings, there was something about him, Brian told me, that made it seem entirely possible. 'I struggle to put it into words – he was ordinary but he was extraordinary,' Brian said.

It was 1961. Brian was twenty-two years old and a student at Manchester Regional College of Art. He took a summer job at A. Monk & Co., then one of the country's biggest construction contractors, engaged in building Britain's post-war infrastructure. It was here, in the delivery yard of the firm's Warrington depot, that Brian met my uncle. Together they hauled scaffolding off and onto lorries, straightening the bent poles in a huge hydraulic machine before returning them to the warehouse. Brian was just passing through in between terms at art college, but for Eric, then twenty-nine years old, this was a permanent gig; the place he had settled after a string of temporary labouring jobs.

Though he had no official authority at Monk – in every job my uncle had, he started at and never rose above the lowest rung – the delivery yard was his domain. It provided him with the nearest thing he ever attained to his own office: a small hut, unheated but offering at least cover from the elements, where he rested between deliveries and from which, according to my dad, he fed a transient population of twenty to thirty feral cats.

Brian remembered the hut and an early – and lasting – impression of my uncle that was formed there. Possibly eager to impress the younger man, Eric asked him, could he do this? Then he leapt up and, with one hand, grabbed an iron beam overhead before gracefully lifting himself up until his chin was resting on the metal. It was the famous one-armed pull-up Buller had told me about. It sounded like a hell of a feat, but I was unsure exactly how hard a one-armed pull-up is. A quick bit of googling led me to a page on bodybuilding.com. The sub-headline of the article – 'Are you up for a strength journey that might take years to complete?' – gave me a fair idea.

Eric had made quite the initial impression on Brian, but it wasn't one that screamed appreciator or practitioner of the arts. So Brian was a little surprised when Eric, on finding out that Brian was an art student, mentioned that he painted. His ambition was to go to St Ives, he said – to live and work there as a painter. 'If I could ever get away from here,' he added, looking around the delivery yard. To Brian's astonishment, the man who unloaded the lorries at A. Monk & Co., who practised one-armed pull-ups in a hut, knew all about the St Ives School, the clique of artists who had made the Cornish fishing town their home. Knew more, in fact, than Brian, the art student.

Nobody else had heard my uncle mention St Ives so I wondered why he'd opened up to Brian about this dream. Perhaps it felt safe to disclose it to someone who was just passing through. It struck me that this was likely the only time in his working life that he met someone who'd been to art school. Someone who wasn't all that

THE DREAMS OF YOUTH

different to him: Brian had briefly worked as a joiner, he told me, and now here they were together in the delivery yard. Perhaps it wasn't so much about how my uncle had related to Brian as how Brian had related to him. He had taken him seriously. He'd been impressed by him and interested. How often, after all, does anyone ask a man in a hut what his dreams are?

I thought about my uncle's postscript: 'If I could ever get away from here.' It felt like it already had the ring of defeat to it, the sense that he felt this dream was unrealisable for him. And with that, perhaps, the feeling that even small steps towards it were out of reach or else pointless. It's a common enough predicament – to find yourself in an unfulfilling job, wondering how you got there, your faith in escaping slipping away. Lugging scaffolding from a hut, my uncle was very much in that place – and before he was even thirty. I wondered how he had found his way here through early adulthood. What were the dreams of his youth? And what were the experiences that weighed heavy on them?

I asked my dad about his earliest memories of his brother making art. He thought about it. He remembered being at his grandmother's house as a child – a typical Victorian two-up two-down, not far from their own. His grandmother called him to come and take a look in the coal hole under the stairs. Peering in, and once his eyes had adjusted, he saw that the walls were covered in drawings: elaborate war scenes and unflattering caricatures of Adolf Hitler. For a time during the war, my uncle and his mother had lived at the house and during air raids, while his mother and grandmother took cover under the kitchen table, he was hidden in here. Perhaps to wrest some control from a frightening experience, he filled the walls with drawings of what he was living through. It seems like a microcosmic foreshadowing of what he went on to spend his life doing.

Eric's friend Buller Crompton remembered him bringing a sketchbook to the boxing club where they trained together as teenagers. 'There was one drawing – of Sugar Ray Robinson – it was so good,' Buller told me, screwing up his face in emphasis. As a teenager, Eric was rarely without a sketchbook in his hand, Buller said.

The school system, as Eric experienced it, was not designed to encourage his talent. It was a time before the state guaranteed free secondary education for all. The curriculum focused on teaching the 'three Rs', with discipline maintained by corporal punishment. Eric frequently played truant, my dad told me, until his education ended at age fourteen and he left school without qualifications.

Born before and educated during the Second World War – for six of my uncle's nine years of schooling the country was at war – he missed out on the widening of opportunities that followed, the so-called 'golden age of social mobility'. To that end, the timing of his birth was remarkably unlucky. In 1944, the eleven-plus exam was introduced, enabling some working-class children to go to grammar school. It was too late for my uncle, who by then was twelve. In 1947, the compulsory school leaving age was raised to fifteen: my uncle's schooling had already ended the year before. By contrast, his workmate,

THE DREAMS OF YOUTH

Brian, just seven years younger, was able to go to art school. Though, like my dad, he studied a vocational subject – the sense of the need to earn a living bearing down that much more acutely on young, working-class minds. Still, it was a world away from the path Eric found himself on.

On leaving school, he began a signwriting apprenticeship, though he never took this up as a job. In fact, my dad thinks he never finished the course, preferring instead to take casual labouring jobs where, in the short term at least, the pay was better. The less you have, the more you're tempted – or forced – to think short-term. Eric's father had died and he may have felt a responsibility to help his mother by contributing more, sooner. Or it might have had as much to do with his character. He craved autonomy and freedom – difficult requirements for a man of his social status.

At this time, as a teenager, Eric's dreams weren't of art but boxing. When his lifelong interest in the sport began, I don't know. But a good guess would be 1942, when two of boxing's biggest names, Joe Louis and Billy Conn – two of the biggest stars in the world, full stop – had an exhibition fight in a park in Warrington. It must have been an unbelievably exciting event for the town, not to mention Eric, then ten years old – the top tier of the sport right in front of his eyes, seeming that much more within reach.

Aged fifteen, he joined a local boxing club. My dad remembered it as a stripped-back room above a pub with a ring and a couple of punch bags, the air thick with the smell of sweat and liniment. It was run by a trainer called Herbie Goulden – a squat man with a flattened nose and a cauliflower ear, his grey hair neatly fixed into an oily central parting. Buller, who joined the club around the same time, described Herbie as 'like a second father'. For Eric, who had lost his own father, he may have been more than that.

Herbie had been a professional timekeeper, responsible for regulating a match's rounds and rest periods, and he ran his club in a dedicated and organised fashion. Buller remembered him turning up late for training just once. 'Sorry lads,' he told them on arriving, 'I was jumped by a gang on my way out the chip shop.' I wondered whether that meant they were aiming to steal Herbie's chips, which seems like the most brilliantly *Beano*-ish mugging. But Herbie, though then in his sixties, had quickly gotten the better of the entire gang, according to Buller. 'Always take out the leader first,' Herbie told his young trainees; it sounded very much like advice Eric might have given me.

Training at the club took place three nights a week, plus a ten-mile run on Sundays. Alongside this, Eric worked jobs on building sites and a stint in a timber yard on the foggy banks of the Manchester Ship Canal, lugging deliveries of wood from barges. I'm amazed he found the energy, outside of this, to train – it's no wonder he could lift his own weight one-handed – but this, I suppose, was his only real shot at a life other than the one prescribed for him.

He began to fight in amateur bouts at clubs, and local

fetes and fairgrounds, my dad told me. This was perhaps, it occurred to me, where his affinity for circus performers and carnival workers began. From there, he somehow found his way into the murky world of unlicensed boxing, drawing his friend Buller in with him.

This was another fact I hadn't known until after my uncle's death, and it was Buller who told me about it. But trying to elicit further details proved tricky. Buller was nervous that the authorities may yet swoop on him. I reassured him that he was probably now safe and he recalled a fight with my uncle in Cheetham Hill, Manchester. There was a thriving underground boxing scene in the area, fuelled by gambling. Eric had fought there before, Buller thought. It was he who had invited his friend along. They fought one another in front of a crowd of maybe one to two thousand people, Buller said. A rabble so raucous that at the end of the match the two friends had to flee through a hatch built into the side of the ring. Eric won the fight, Buller recalled, commending his left hook. But at the time, they were more concerned about the sizeable portion of the crowd who had bet on the wrong outcome and were now baying for their blood.

This can't have been what my uncle dreamed of when he first put on a pair of gloves. They did it because 'you could earn a week's wages in a night,' Buller explained. The lure of ready cash had once again proved too tempting. But it seems that Eric managed to get his boxing aspirations back on track – or at least, he tried to. In 1950, two months before his eighteenth birthday, he received his professional licence under the name 'Jack Flowers'. We found this among all the stuff in his house – a small, leather-bound wallet containing licence papers and a suitably surly mugshot. Along with it were stacks of old boxing magazines and photo-cards of fighters – the ghosts of teenage ambition. That sense that, in lieu of a clear strategy, madly collecting the paraphernalia will manifest the dream.

Why he took a ring name, we don't know. Perhaps to make a clean break from his unlicensed fights. He created it, I suspect, by amalgamating the names of Jack Johnson and Tiger Flowers, two Black American champions. In a time of overt racism, particularly within the sport, white fans generally always supported white fighters. But my uncle had no truck with that. He backed the fighter he considered the best – or the underdog. Very often, they were one and the same. 'The best fighter is a hungry fighter,' he used to say, and I think that was a big part of what he loved about the sport: to have nothing, and so nothing to lose, was an advantage.

But here again, the timing of Eric's birth proved extraordinarily unlucky. In 1949, national service came into force, a compulsory eighteen-month period in the armed forces for young men. That same year, my uncle turned seventeen, the age of conscription – though he was actually called up a year later. Soldiers weren't permitted to box professionally so this put a halt to that. Given that fact, I wondered why he had bothered to apply for his licence at this time. Perhaps he had made the application before he was called up. Or perhaps he did it as a promise to himself, in an effort to hold on to this dream during his time away. He would continue to box as an amateur in the army – and sketch – but for the most part, army life was not an experience he would relish. If his need for personal freedom had rubbed up against his social circumstances to this point, then it was about to collide with a brick wall.

Eric was dispatched to barracks in Catterick, North Yorkshire – an area that seemed to a young man from an industrial town like a desolate wilderness. The barracks themselves were a 'hellhole' by his description, and he wasn't exactly used to luxury. After six weeks of basic training, he was assigned to the Royal Horse Guards at their base in Windsor.

If the short, sharp shock of his training was meant to instil discipline in my uncle, it seems to have instead roused his rebellious spirit. At the barracks in Windsor, he developed a habit of 'going over the wall': disappearing after dark to nearby London to enjoy the nightlife – on one occasion to watch British boxer Randy Turpin beat the legendary Sugar Ray Robinson. As a result, he received more than one trip to 'the glasshouse' – military prison, a prescription of solitary confinement and sometimes forced labour, delivered with a sprinkling of sadism.

Eric never spoke in any detail about these spells in detention. It's likely they were brief, given his offences were relatively minor, but I don't doubt they were nonetheless grim, even traumatic experiences. Just a few years earlier, there had been riots at two separate detention barracks in protest at the harsh conditions.

From Windsor, his regiment was posted to West Germany, occupying an old SS base close to the border with East Germany. Eric told us the story of his first night there. Exhausted from their journey, he and his fellow soldiers were woken after what seemed like five minutes' sleep. 'The Russians are coming!' their sergeant bellowed. They had to briskly pack up not only their belongings but the entire camp, leaving no trace of their brief occupation. Everything, including the officers' silverware, went back into the trucks from where it had not long been unloaded. In the depths of night, they left the barracks and started travelling west. After what felt like several hours on the road, the officers stopped them. They were informed that this had been an exercise and ordered to turn back.

Whatever faith Eric had in the army's systems and processes, it was, at this point, destroyed. He believed himself to be under the command of madmen. And so, on returning to the barracks, he took to living in an abandoned building he'd spotted on the peripheries of the base. He would turn up to the NAAFI – the army canteen – every morning, but not to parade; his own kind of pick 'n' mix version of military life. He continued to live like this until he felt sufficiently comfortable to deign to return to parading. Astonishingly, nobody with any seniority noticed his absence nor his return. It was one occasion, at least, when he escaped the glasshouse.

My uncle wasn't against military life – at least not until he experienced it. Far from it, he had wanted to follow in the footsteps of his father: to join the 12th Lancers and serve as a driver of armoured vehicles, which must have seemed particularly exciting to someone who had never been in a car. Although he was assigned to the

Horse Guards, he did learn to drive armoured vehicles there. Though this came to an abrupt end one day when he accidentally crushed a civilian car. Luckily, the car was empty, but the experience shook him. He got out of his vehicle and, when an officer ordered him to get back inside, he refused. And so off to the glasshouse he went.

Following this, he was given a role that better suited him – in the cookhouse, where he remained for the rest of his service, enjoying a fair degree of freedom. My dad remembered his brother saying how, often, on night duty, he had the run of the place, frying up steak and sausages for friends. It reminded me a little of our late-evening cheese-on-toast sessions on holiday in Pembrokeshire. They had a run-of-the-cookhouse energy as my uncle, bookmaker's pen tucked behind his ear, raided the fridge for cheddar and commandeered the grill. There were further benefits to the cookhouse job. If the same friends he'd supplied with fry-ups were on guard duty after he'd taken a trip over the wall, then he could waltz back in with impunity. It seems that, eventually, Eric found his niche in the army.

One excursion – possibly over the wall – that Eric made while stationed in Germany was a tale he liked to tell. Hearing that the Harlem Globetrotters, the world-famous basketball team, were appearing in nearby Hanover, he attempted to hitch a ride to see them. He spent a while by the side of the road with his thumb out, watching car after car drive by. He was about to give up hope when a coach pulled over. Climbing aboard, he told the driver he was trying to get to town for the Globetrotters' game. 'Us too,' the driver said, pointing to his passengers – who my uncle then realised were the Harlem Globetrotters. They gave him a ride plus a free ticket to the show, he said.

Truthfully, I was never really sure I believed this story – along with a number of my uncle's tales. He seemed to have an unending reserve of these wild claims. Example: I once picked up a small obituary, torn from an old newspaper, in his living room – a local character, he told me, a man he'd known in his youth. After giving me crucial facts about this man, like which pubs he used to drink in and just how hard he was – I was about ten at the time, by the way – he casually added, as an afterthought, that the man had fought alongside Buffalo Bill. Another example, thematically related, it occurs to me: for years he maintained we had American Indian blood. Sometimes spoken with a twinkle in his eye, sometimes with such seriousness that he seemed genuinely offended if questioned. So I filed the Harlem Globetrotters claim alongside many others of spurious veracity. Perhaps he'd seen them play but, really, what were the chances they'd picked him up as a hitchhiker? Then after his death, we found a small autograph book in his house. And in it, the signatures of several players in the 1951 line-up of the Globetrotters. Shortly after, I took a DNA test.

Eric's military service ended with one final act of defiance. He returned home for Christmas, my dad recalled, with his kitbag completely filled with meat – meat he had stolen from the officers' private larder, the spoils of a hunting trip in the forests of Lower Saxony. He had brought it all the way from Germany, only nearly finding himself compromised when the bag started leaking blood at Euston station. With post-war rationing still in force, meat of such quality and quantity was like treasure. The family and half the street ate well, my dad said, laughing. It was a parting act of revenge for the midnight evacuation and all the trips to the glasshouse.

In its efforts to instil unquestioning respect for authority, the army seems to have achieved in Eric the exact opposite. It may have also inspired what became a lifelong habit of his: petty theft. I remember how, faced with a bowl of salt or sugar sachets at a café, a couple would go on his tray, a fistful would go in his pocket. And sometimes a second in mine. Not wishing to incriminate a dead man, let's just say this attitude extended to further interactions with other organisations and institutions. In life, as in the army, I think he felt at the mercy of a basically mad and unfair system, and saw this as a minor redressing of the balance.

The habit continued when, returned from the army, he found work at a local brewery. My dad remembered him cycling home, his bicycle teetering because every pocket of his substantial overcoat, inside and out, contained pilfered bottles of beer. One night, as my dad lay in bed, the silence was shattered, he said, by a prolonged smashing of glass on the cobbles outside his window. His brother had fallen off his bike.

On his return from the army, Eric also resumed training at the local boxing club. Managed by Herbie, he had a handful of fights – most of which he won, my dad thought – before hanging up his gloves. His boxing licence appears to have lapsed when he was twenty-two. He described himself as a 'reactive fighter' – a counter-puncher – who lacked an innate aggression he deemed necessary to go further. But my dad thought Eric's giving up the sport had more to do with the emotional toll he saw it taking on their mother. However, it seems to me that his national service also stole the momentum from his teenage dream. It convinced him that he wasn't a fighter – and this wasn't wrong. The realisation made way for another dream to begin to sow its seeds. One that felt less probable but more true.

Painting didn't arrive quickly for my uncle. He bumbled along for a while, living his life. He established his group of drinking buddies at the Cross Keys. He got a new job as a gravedigger at the town's main cemetery. He avoided factory work, my dad believed, because he needed to be outside and he didn't like answering to a foreman. By those measures, gravedigging suited him. But he eventually gave it up and returned to casual labouring after having to dig a child's grave. 'He was too soft, my brother,' my dad said, shaking his head; proof, given he'd survived military detention and unlicensed boxing rings, that sensitivity and toughness are by no means mutually exclusive.

He continued to draw and he began to dabble in paint but it wasn't until some years later, when he reached his late twenties, that the 'painting bug got really into my bloodstream', as he had told the *Liverpool Echo*. Before this, he had another experience that seems to have shaped him, one that would appear to have been an integral precursor to his creative outpouring. At around twenty-seven years old, he left home and moved to South Wales for a little over a year, to labour on the construction of the great steelworks at Llanwern. This was something else I hadn't known about my uncle until my dad mentioned it in his eulogy. It was a difficult time in his life, I later discovered, a period somewhat shrouded in secrecy.

I asked my dad what he knew about his brother's time in South Wales. He told me that he had lived for a time in Tiger Bay, the dockside area of Cardiff that was a byword for danger and illicit activities. He slept in a cheap boarding house there – the kind of place where as one man leaves his bed to go to work, another returning takes it. There was a bus that, at the crack of dawn, shuttled workers to the site. Beyond these scant facts, he hadn't shared much about his time in Tiger Bay, my dad said, though he'd loved the area, of that my dad felt sure.

In lieu of more details, I watched some old film footage on YouTube and read some articles, trying to get a sense of what life in Tiger Bay was like when my uncle was there in the late 1950s. More often than not, in interviews, people seemed to be falling over themselves to say it really wasn't that bad – which made me think it must have been quite bad. I watched a black-and-white interview with a surprisingly posh English lady who appeared to be drunk. She recalled cafés full of prostitutes and policemen stabbed. 'But it's lovely now,' she insisted slurringly.

The truth may be that Tiger Bay both deserved its reputation and didn't. It had been a major coal-exporting port, a bustling, international junction with a transient population of merchant seamen. An area whose tone is largely set by the urges of late nineteenth-century sailors is bound to have a certain flavour. Men confined together for weeks at sea were suddenly released onto dry land with a few free hours to exorcise their pent-up energies. A sub-economy of brothels and gambling, drinking and opium dens emerged to service them. Fights and violence were common. Murders would go unsolved because the perpetrators had sailed away before the police could catch them. But among the fleeting visitors, some began to settle and a multinational, multiethnic community blossomed.

By the time Eric arrived, coal exports had fallen and unemployment was rising. Tiger Bay retained its air of chaos, its reputation now firmly though not necessarily fairly established. There were nearly a hundred pubs in the area, with nicknames like the Bucket of Blood and the Snakepit. One was apparently known as the Six Tits in honour of the three barmaids who served there – and giving a good sense of the pub's policy on sexual harassment. But there were also bohemian vibes to be found, with live jazz and international cuisine on offer. As well as, by most accounts, a close-knit resident community. Inspired by a visit to Tiger Bay, poet Gwyn Thomas wrote, 'Whenever any two children of different races play together, humanity grows an inch or two; another ancient fear, another mouldering prejudice is told to mind its manners and behave.' All life was there, living vigorously among crumbling grey buildings salt-bitten by sea air and drizzle – the whole, mad world in a few square miles. Perhaps that's what people meant when they were trying to describe the area: yes, it was bad but it was good.

The more I learned about Tiger Bay, the more it sounded like the landscape of my uncle's dreams; the chief inspiration behind his exhortations for me to steer clear of fancy living and instead seek out the dive bars and insalubrious drinking dens. Had he found his spiritual home in Tiger Bay? Or had the place shaped his character? Perhaps it was a little of both.

Tiger Bay, now the redeveloped Cardiff Bay, isn't so far from St Ives in the grand scheme of things: head west towards open water, take a left at the mouth of the Bristol Channel and you're almost there. But in every other sense, for my uncle, sleeping in little more than a doss house, bussed each day to a sprawling construction site for a shift of hard labour, it was a million miles away. That said, though it may have lacked the light and tranquillity of the Cornish fishing town, it had much else to offer a fledgling artist in its verve and vivacity. Was it here that my uncle began to dream of being a painter? If not, it was shortly upon his return. Because this was when he suddenly began to create art in manic abundance. It was also when he got his job in the delivery yard of A. Monk and Co. He had begun to hear his calling. And at the same time, his life had delivered him, by every turn, to a place where fulfilling it seemed impossible.

While my dad was in the early stages of cataloguing Eric's work, in his cluttered, end-of-terrace house in Warrington, I was two hundred miles away in London on the set of a TV show I'd co-written. One day, there was someone by the monitors I didn't recognise. She was on a scheme, she said, to help young people from low-income families gain experience in the industry. That's good, I thought, followed by a sense of dismay that a scheme like this is necessary in a medium that's all about mass communication.

Looking out at the crew, it occurred to me that, in terms of social make-up, I probably could have been looking at a film crew in the 1930s: top-level roles were largely filled by people with private educations. From there down, most people were state-educated and middle class, until you reached the lowest-status (but often far from lowest-skilled) jobs. Those in the top roles weren't undeserving of them exactly – they were talented, hard-working people. Then again, I've known many talented, hard-working people who haven't caught such breaks, not least my uncle.

Privilege delivers a more direct link between effort and reward – indeed, any link at all. The sense that hard work can – will, even – lead to something, as opposed to just being what you do to survive. The belief in that link might be even more important than its existence, though clearly one feeds the other. People have sometimes told me how private schools cultivate their students to expect to be the leaders of tomorrow, stated as if it were a simple, powerful technique that the state sector would do well to learn from, conveniently overlooking the fact that it's also an accurate appraisal of the status quo. To see that others like us have already trodden the path clearly gives us confidence that we could too. More than that, it can be the catalyst of a dream in itself. I'm sure this was a large part of why Eric pursued boxing. It was the one place he saw young men like him making a name for themselves. Like football later, it was the only dream readily available to the working classes.

Of course, there were working-class artists of my uncle's generation who built careers for themselves: Hockney, for example, and Peter Blake. My uncle didn't feel much – if any – affinity with either of them, I'm certain. Unlike him, they had been afforded the chance to stay in education, and attend their local art school, from where their talents took them to the Royal College of Art. Also, growing up, Hockney's father was an office clerk; Blake's was an electrician, and his mother a nurse. These were skilled, comparatively well-paid jobs. (Their fathers were also, crucially, alive.) My point is that to someone like my uncle, even these artists – the ones who had defied the odds – seemed relatively well-to-do.

There was one artist at the time whom I suspect Eric felt an affinity with – a northern painter, ten years older than him, called Alan Lowndes. ('Lowndes', by coincidence, was also my grandmother's maiden name.) Now somewhat and unfairly forgotten, he was then quite well known. Eric certainly knew of him, according to my dad – and I suspect his work may have influenced my uncle just as much as, or perhaps even more than, Lowry's. Lowndes's father was a railway clerk – a white-collar job – but, like Eric, he had left school at fourteen. He lived and worked for a time in St Ives, though he was never really considered part of the St Ives set. Had this been the inspiration for my uncle's dream?

These artists were part of what is now seen as a 'golden age' for working-class voices in the arts. Established creatives from working-class backgrounds have since lamented its decline. Currently, of my generation, less than 8 per cent of creative workers are from a working-class background.* (In my experience, that figure seems generous.) Set that against 48 per cent of the public who consider themselves working class.†

In fact, a study published by the British Sociological Association claims those figures have actually remained consistent relative to one another over the past fifty years; that access to creative work has consistently been 'profoundly unequal in class terms'. In other words, there was no golden age.

Still, there are times when working-class voices at least feel more present. As a teenager in the 1990s, I watched Jarvis Cocker on *Top of the Pops* singing about 'how it feels to live your life with no meaning or control'; Liam Gallagher swaggering up to collect Brit awards. It seemed like every band wanted to claim working-class credentials. I read an article where even Radiohead had half a crack at it. And almost as audaciously, I went to school wearing one of my uncle's donkey jackets. It seemed to me, then, like the inevitable march of progress; then, as time went on, more like a blip. It's telling that these all-too-brief periods are often heralded as purple patches in British cultural life. What, in the meantime, have we been missing? Telling too, perhaps, that they emerged explosively, with a sense of latent talent and energy bursting out when finally given the opportunity – or when feeling empowered to take it.

---

* According to ONS data analysed by the authors of 'Social Mobility and "Openness" in Creative Occupations since the 1970s', 2022.
† According to data from the Social Mobility Commission's 'Social Mobility Barometer', 2021.

THE DREAMS OF YOUTH

Eric was born into a people whose dreams weren't expected to be realised or their hard work rewarded. He wasn't given much you could describe as an opportunity – little education, no chance to go to art school. But more than that, I think the experiences of his formative years inoculated him against ever feeling comfortable or confident in such a place. It was these years, I think, that shaped his lifelong mistrust of middle-class people – one so ingrained that, to a degree, it even extended to me. They caned him, they stuck him in the army, they made him march through the night in fear of attack, they threw him in the glasshouse when he was suffering from shock. He framed these events as humorous anecdotes – I don't think he necessarily felt they'd been traumatic, which wasn't a word in his vocabulary. But I can also imagine him sharply setting right anyone who appeared to underestimate their unpleasantness. Certainly, they entrenched in him a sense of 'us and them'. Art colleges, universities, private art galleries, and a great many other environments he was wary of – meaning, I think, anywhere he was unlikely to be met as an equal: this was the world of 'them'. And he was unwilling to make a single adjustment to himself to fit in it.

There were two irreconcilable destinies set within my uncle: to be an artist and to be nothing of the sort. He was both the man in the hut and the man dreaming of St Ives, and not necessarily one more than the other. He was both, and there's no reason he shouldn't have been, but in the world as it was – as it is – they couldn't easily coexist as a whole. At least not publicly.

A little while after the email from Brian came a further intriguing discovery. We found evidence, stuffed in one of the plastic bags that dotted Eric's painting room, that he had entered the local open-call exhibition before the year of his win – apparently without telling anyone. It briefly felt like a minor revelation: perhaps he wasn't such a secret artist. Then the irony struck me that I was only finding this out now because he'd done it so covertly. I wondered why. In tentatively opening up, it was perhaps a way of maintaining close control of the situation. It gave a little more context to his belated wish for an exhibition, I thought. This must surely have been when that desire manifested, though it took him more than twenty years to say it out loud. It seems as if the real secret in my uncle's life – the thing most deeply hidden, that had taken longer to unearth than all of his paintings – was his ambition.

The experiences of his adolescence and young adulthood explain a lot about Eric, the difficulties he faced as an artist, both in the world and in himself. But not everything. He had a vulnerability around his work that seems to me to go beyond this. It was part of a wider fragility that can't just be put down to a sensitive, artistic temperament or even the injustices of class. It was the reason for his binding attachment to his mother and, I think, why he'd never found love. And perhaps also why painting became so essential for him – something he had to do. The causes, I discovered, lie in the story of his childhood, with its traumatic events and their lifelong repercussions. His strange, difficult living situation, and his turbulent relationship with his stepfather. The reason why he exiled himself to South Wales. The story of how he almost split the family in two.

CHAPTER 11

THE OTHER ERIC TUCKER

Eric was born in Warrington, Lancashire in 1932 to parents Eric and Joan. His father was a greengrocer's assistant, his mother a domestic servant – or 'skivvy' as they were called. Joan was actually my grandmother's middle name but she considered her first name, Susannah, too awful to use. Even the local doctor had reprimanded her mother for choosing it, she claimed.

Both she and her husband had lost parents at a young age. Eric Senior was an orphan by the time he was thirteen, and my grandmother's father died in an industrial accident when she was nineteen. As a result, my uncle's immediate family, growing up, was small: his two parents, plus his maternal grandmother, Granny Lowndes. Theirs were the three portraits that hung in his living room at the end of his life.

He and his parents lived in Hume Street, a long, straight road of flat-fronted terraced houses with a corner shop at one end and a factory – a wire works – at the other. Warrington had been a thriving industrial centre in the nineteenth century and wire production was one of its main industries. It even provided the town's rugby team with its nickname: the Wire. By the time of my uncle's birth, it was still an industrial town but the Great Depression was in full effect; the country was at the peak of a severe and persistent unemployment crisis, with the north of England particularly badly hit.

We don't know much about Eric's early years. But my dad, who was born nine years later and grew up in the same house, maintains that daily life was much the same for him as a child as it was for his brother. In fact, he contends that not much had changed in working-class life since the Victorian era. At home, they had no central heating and no bathroom. The toilet was a short, cold walk to the end of the yard, not connected to sewers but emptied in the small hours by 'night soil men' – a job title that seems purpose-made to terrify children.

The family lived in a Victorian-built house and inhabited it in a Victorian way. There were two bedrooms upstairs and, downstairs, a parlour at the rear – where the family lived, cooked, ate, and bathed – and a front room kept for special occasions. There were no cars, or at least they knew nobody who owned one. This meant my grandmother could chuck the family dog out onto the street each morning. My dad would occasionally see it, he said, out and about in the streets or nearby fields, mooching around or scrapping with another dog.

There was no National Health Service so calls and visits to the doctor were avoided. When someone died, there was an oldish lady around the corner who came and dealt with the scene: the 'laying out' of the body. It wasn't an official job but a matriarchal role she'd somehow come to assume.

There were characters and practices like this hanging on from the previous century. Like a knife sharpener man, my dad recalled, who toured the cobbled streets on a bike with a stone wheel attached, which he pressed housewives' kitchen knives to. And the local rag and bone man with his horse and cart, who announced his arrival with an enigmatic – and frankly spooky – cry of 'Kee-bo-bo'.

I was eventually convinced of my dad's quasi-Victorian childhood when he mentioned how, during cinema screenings – the Saturday matinee – the manager would travel down the aisle with a 'flit gun', spraying the audience of kids with an unknown substance. Possibly a lice treatment, my dad thought, though he never actually knew what it was. Nor much cared as the cowboy picture started. The invention of cinema aside, something about that experience spoke to me of a Victorian mindset: the casual understanding, by all involved, that a crowd of children must be fumigated.

Listening to these memories, I realised that my dad was very much describing the world of his brother's paintings – his street scenes, at least; largely empty of vehicles but full of chattering housewives, roaming dogs and rag and bone men. The street furniture of these scenes – concrete bollards and lampposts – date them to the time they were painted, but the characters often look to be from a previous era. There's a similar effect in Lowry's work and it was a feeling I think my uncle connected with. In some ways it's just a true observation: modernity doesn't descend like a blanket, it filters through – to some people and places much more slowly. But I think there was more to it than this for my uncle. He was a little glued to the world of his childhood – it was a time he needed to keep alive, a place where he had unresolved business.

Two tragedies hit the family when Eric was young. His parents had a second child, Peter, born shortly before my uncle's fifth birthday, who died of pneumonia at just eight months old. Peter's existence was unknown to me until I researched family records while writing this book. It wasn't a part of my dad's argument, but it adds grim credence to his claim that life for working-class families hadn't changed much since the Victorian era.

The second tragedy occurred when my uncle was ten. War had been declared two years earlier and the following year his father had been called up to join the army. In the summer of 1942, a couple of months after my uncle's tenth birthday, his mother received a telegram informing her that her husband had been killed in action.

Neither of these tragedies was uncommon at the time, though that can't have made them any less devastating to experience. In some ways, perhaps it made it worse – you felt less permitted to see such profound losses as anything particularly remarkable.

Following her husband's death, my grandmother was left to care for my uncle and his eight-month-old brother: my dad, born after his father had set off for war. She took in a lodger and got a job at a nearby paper factory. She had help from her mother, and her brother, Jim, would sometimes take young Eric on fishing trips to North Wales.

My grandmother always seemed to me an easy-going

lady. She had a languid way of speaking and a slow blink. She liked a laugh. She seemed relaxed and untroubled by life, but she had certainly had her share to be troubled by. Aside from losing a child and then her husband, she had an older brother, Billy, who had suffered a breakdown. He was sent to the local psychiatric hospital where he remained for the rest of his life. A talented musician, he never spoke but would sometimes sing as he played the piano. It was Billy's fading music certificate, I realised, that Eric kept framed on his bedroom wall. According to my dad, their mother took two buses to visit her brother and bring him sandwiches every week for fifty years. Sometimes when she visited, he had bruises or a black eye. Self-inflicted, hospital staff assured her; the result of an accident. She didn't believe them. But as a working-class woman faced with better-educated professionals, she saw no recourse for action. On top of this, later, two of her children – my dad and my aunt – contracted tuberculosis and spent long periods convalescing far from home. Little wonder she became so depressed that she was given electroshock therapy.

Eric had been the one to live through most of these experiences with his mother. And it was this fact, and perhaps the fear of losing another parent, that I think bound him to her; that ingrained in him a need to be close to and care for her. Day to day, this mostly meant keeping her spirits up. But strangely, it could occasionally mean the very opposite. I remember how, at any mention of Billy, my uncle would reflexively raise his terrible treatment at the hospital and how much it had hurt his mother. He said this in front of her as if doing her a courtesy, which she seemed to take it as. He was sharing her burdens, making sure they weren't overlooked. But ironically, my uncle's devotion to his mother became one of the very burdens – perhaps over time *the* greatest – that she had to bear.

Less than four years after his father's death, Eric entered the working world. The war had ended. Shortly after this, my grandmother's life took a happier turn: she met and fell in love with Bert Urey, the man I would later call Grandad. He was younger than her, with dark, slicked-back hair and an easy smile. He worked with his brother, travelling around town with a handcart, pasting up billboard advertisements. They married in 1947 and Bert moved into the family home. But it was a union that my uncle, then a teenager, had trouble accepting – to say the least.

Throughout his life, Eric exalted a small number of close relatives to a status beyond reproach – 'The Holy Family', as my dad referred to them with an eye roll. They included Eric's mother, his father, Granny Lowndes, my dad, Uncle Billy, and 'to some extent' Uncle Jim. Everyone else was met with some degree of suspicion. Even his half-sister, my aunt, though he undoubtedly loved her, wasn't quite admitted to the clique. These were the relatives who had populated my uncle's life before the death of his father, I realised. It was as if everyone who arrived thereafter was at fault simply for personifying the march of time. But none more so than Bert.

Eric resented his stepfather's presence from the outset.

It must have been difficult to see another man step into the space from which his father had been wrenched. And the fact that Bert, though he'd been in the army, hadn't seen active service may have stoked the bitter feelings. Though of course neither of these things was Bert's fault.

The resentment bubbled away. 'Whatever Bert did, he couldn't win,' my mum explained to me. Bert's sister tried to reassure him that his surly teenage stepson was 'just a monkey'. But given my uncle was bigger and taller than Bert, and increasingly proficient at boxing, I can't imagine this description quite landed for him.

Eric's national service promised some respite for Bert. And the reasonable hope that his stepson might be leaving home for good. But of course, he wasn't. After leaving the army, my uncle returned to the family home where by now there was a new baby, my aunt. On top of this, Bert had established a good relationship with my dad who, never having known his own father, was able to take Bert as he found him – a kind and loving stepdad. My uncle had come home to find a new version of the family – one getting on very well without him. Where once Bert had been the outsider, Eric's time away had turned the tables.

The five of them lived together in a house with just two bedrooms – my dad and his brother in one room; my grandmother, Bert, and the baby in the other. Slowly but surely following Eric's return, the tensions resumed – and proceeded to mount with gusto. Until, one evening at the kitchen table, there was an explosive row between my uncle and his stepfather. With post-war rationing still in place, food was a rather scarce commodity, and Eric became obsessed with ensuring his younger brother was receiving his fair share; his implication being that Bert would otherwise favour his daughter.

Eric accused his stepfather of some perceived show of favouritism and a furious shouting match ensued. Of course, like all blazing rows, it wasn't really about what it was about. It was the moment when years of simmering antipathy finally boiled over. Every harboured grudge between the two men was suddenly, fervidly voiced. Afterwards, there was a tense, unpleasant atmosphere in the house, my dad said. He recalled coming home from school in the days following to find his mother in tears. He avoided the house, he said, playing out in the streets for as long as he could.

Not long after this, Bert left and went to live at his mother's. He had planned to take his daughter with him but, in the end, he didn't – it was a step too far. But the fact that he left without her is testament to how unbearable things had become for him. Or perhaps, as my uncle might contend, it was a move calculated to produce the results it did: after persuading her husband to return, my grandmother told Eric he would have to go.

Eric was heartbroken. Likely his mother was too. Perhaps it seemed like she had chosen his stepfather over him but, in the circumstances, there wasn't much else she could do. She had a child to raise and Eric was now a young man in his twenties. Hearing of work going in South Wales, he took it. I wonder if there was a degree of theatre to this relocation; an attempt to upstage his stepfather's earlier decampment. But I don't doubt that my uncle was genuinely cut up. This was when he had written the letter to his mother – the letter my dad had lost – in which he spoke of his great loneliness.

As with his national service, Eric's time away provided the family with a period of much-needed respite from the tensions. But as with his national service, when the job ended, he returned once again to the house. This time, for good. If Bert had hoped to force his wife to choose between living with him or with her eldest son, he may have inadvertently set a challenge for my uncle, who would do something precisely because there was pressure on him to do the opposite. Here began an epic battle of wills between two men who were, unfortunately, quite evenly matched.

By then, the family had moved to King George Crescent: a larger council house with three bedrooms and a bathroom. It was not long after Eric's return that my dad contracted tuberculosis, followed by his sister. When it was time for my aunt to come home from the sanatorium, the doctor advised that she needed her own room – she should no longer share with her parents. So, Eric moved. Not out, but downstairs, taking over the front parlour as his bedroom; a sure sign he had no plans to leave.

If Eric hoped his younger brother, as 'blood family', might join him in his feud, he was to be severely disappointed. Aside from the fact that my dad loved his stepfather, another turn of events in the years to come would bring the two families – the Tuckers and the Ureys – even closer; a double knot in the union. My dad would fall in love with and marry Bert's niece, my mum. My uncle, in his resentment, in his failure to accept the passage of events, would find himself more isolated than ever.

It seems to me no coincidence that, not long after his return from Wales, Eric's art-making exploded into action. He had arrived at a place where he could see what the rest of his life looked like, and it wasn't enough. His job in the delivery yard, for one. Also, returning home for the second time, he must have had some sense that this was it, he wasn't going to leave. Perhaps also that he might never find a partner. I wonder if, in his time away, he had made some peace with his aloneness, gained more of a sense of himself that pointed him towards art and the lives of those who made it. But I think there was something else.

'The urge to paint seemed to come up suddenly' was the way he had described it in the *Liverpool Echo* article. He makes it sound like some force overtook him – bubbled up from within – that he can't quite explain. It seems to me that the traumatic events of his childhood, in particular the death of his father, must have been a major catalyst in this. And the isolation he felt as a result, even within his own family. He was carrying so much inside, and by himself, that when he turned his attention to creative expression, the floodgates opened. Drawing and art were things he'd long been interested in, but then they became necessary.

Even his painting room was established around this time. When my dad left home and Eric was able to take his bedroom, he had already filled the front room with paintings, effectively claiming it for good. It was a remarkable sacrifice by my grandparents – and not exactly a choice. But it allowed them to establish the back room as their domain, representing something like the life they might have expected to live together. Eric didn't quite have a place in that room, it occurs to me. They each took an armchair; he tended to perch on a small wooden chair by the door. His uneasiness in the house was surely part of what led him to spend so many hours alone in his painting room – making images that, ironically, seem to celebrate togetherness and community. The isolation he felt was perhaps why he so valued those aspects of working-class life.

Some years after my dad left home, his younger sister followed. They left to make their own homes and families, leaving their older brother behind. And so the configuration at King George Crescent was set, for all the years that followed: Eric, his mother and Bert. An uneasy truce settled between the two men. They learned to live separately, together. With an invisible wall between them, they almost moved around the house like ghosts who couldn't see one another.

Occasionally over the years, tensions flared up – in increasingly abstruse ways. My dad recalled a time when Eric became convinced that his stepfather was trying to psyche him out by uncrossing and recrossing his legs whenever Eric spoke. It sounds like a crazy accusation but it wasn't necessarily wrong, my dad thought. Though his brother's foibles were more palpable, 'Bert was no angel either,' he said.

There was one final flare-up, which my aunt remembered. It was around the same time as the leg-crossing accusation and possibly related. Things came to a head when the three of them visited her house in Oxfordshire. She believed it was to do with Eric's recent acquisition of a car – though by this point it was probably impossible for anyone on the outside to fully understand what was going on. My dad had given his brother his old car, hoping to gift him some independence. But in what increasingly feels like a Pinteresque comedy of menace, it proved a weapon in the cold war between my uncle and Bert. The car, and Eric's sole ability to drive it, afforded him a new power over his stepfather. Even its configuration, with my uncle in the driving seat, his mother next to him, and Bert in the back, may have piqued Bert – an upending of the hierarchy subtly suggested by the seating arrangements in their back room. Whatever the details, Bert reached the end of his tether and once again moved out – this time to his sister's house. And again, after a little while, he was persuaded to return and the uneasy truce resumed.

They lived like this, astonishingly, for some forty-five years in total – until Bert died. Even now, in death, the unlikely trio remain together. In accordance with both men's presumed wish to be beside my grandmother, all three share a cemetery plot and memorial stone. The circle – or rather triangle – proved as impossible to square in eternity as it had been in life.

In a couple of my uncle's drawings, both of dominoes games, I noticed that one of the players bore a striking resemblance to my grandad Bert. I was amazed. Was this just a coincidence or an unconscious act? Or was it, I wondered, a surprising tribute by my uncle to his supposed nemesis? Whichever the case, it caused me to think that Eric, at times, must have felt self-conscious – maybe even sympathetic – about the challenge he presented to his stepfather. My dad recalled how hurt his brother had once been by a terse exchange he'd had with a neighbour he didn't get on with. Eric was 'the cuckoo who never flew the nest', the neighbour had sneered over the garden wall, getting the saying wrong but still making his point and landing a blow.

It was difficult not to see Eric as the cause of the problems with his stepfather and their impossible domestic situation – as the grown son who just wouldn't leave home. But he was more unable than unwilling to go, I believe. He was tough enough to deal with a lot of things – hard labour, military detention and unlicensed boxing rings – so the forces influencing this must have been considerable.

In Eric's painting room, in the drawer where he kept mementoes pleasant and painful, there were a few small photographs of his father: the other Eric Tucker. He's a handsome man, rake-thin with a tall shock of *Eraserhead* hair; a young husband and father in his late twenties.

Alongside the photographs, we found a short letter that Eric, aged nine, had written to his father while he was at war. It must have been returned with his father's possessions after his death. The spelling is so bad, and the dip pen ink so splodgy, that the note is hardly decipherable – except for 'Dear dad' at the top and, at the bottom, 'from Eric' followed by, I counted, twenty-six inky kisses. But the page of lined paper, which looks like it was torn from a school exercise book, is mostly filled with a drawing: the earliest example we have of a piece of art by my uncle.

It is a battlefield scene with a saluting soldier front and centre: his father. In the background, a howitzer fires a missile through the air, while a little plane crashes to the ground with a cry of 'achtung'. He's visualising what his father is living. He's there with him. Looking at the drawing, it struck me that, for a child with a father at war, a clever imagination might be an unfortunate gift.

A smaller character in the drawing is labelled 'Lesley Tucker' – his father's younger brother. It is as if my uncle is reminding his dad that he's not out there alone. Or perhaps he's reminding himself. The whole effect is to make war seem a little friendlier.

Not having experienced this as a child – my dad going off to war – I would have imagined the intense yearning would be for him not to go, or to come back home. But looking at this drawing, it occurred to me that it may be to go along with him. That more distressing than him being there, is your not being there with him.

I asked my dad what he knew about their father's death. He was killed in the Western Desert of Egypt, my dad said, in the lead-up to the First Battle of El Alamein. According to what his brother had told him, their father was driving a light-armoured car when his squad got caught in a sandstorm. When the storm cleared, they found themselves surrounded by a Panzer tank division, completely outgunned. They were fired on – didn't stand a chance. My uncle had the idea that his father, shot to pieces, was deserted by his fellow men. That he was given morphine by German soldiers but ultimately left to die.

Eric's belief that his father had been deserted or forgotten was one which seemed to haunt him. And not without further cause. Though she was informed of her husband's death by the standard telegram, my grandmother did not receive the customary commanding officer's letter, with a full explanation of the circumstances of her husband's death, until a year or more later. It came with an apology and an insistence that letters had been sent – an insistence my uncle mistrusted. And when the names of fallen soldiers were added to the town's war memorial, Eric Tucker's name was missed. The oversight, which extended to a handful of other names, was eventually corrected – fifty years later. It was so long after the fact that I was alive and old enough to remember it. It was a tremendously important occasion for my uncle – the one time, up until then, that I'd really seen him dress up smart. I realise now it was the first time he had attended any kind of memorial service for his father – there had been no funeral and he had no grave to visit.

Growing up, there was little to no mention of their father in the house, my dad said, and he didn't think to ask. My grandmother had remarried. She had moved on. But in doing so, she left her son behind. Because the loss of his father inflicted an emotional wound on my uncle from which he never really recovered, from which he never moved on. It was an experience he seemed to palpably carry about him even into old age.

At the end of his life, he told my dad that his one real fear in dying was their father being forgotten. As if, for him, the more significant thing about his own death was that it meant a kind of final erasure of his father. It spoke to me of the tremendous personal duty he'd felt to maintain a sense of his father's existence. Perhaps by determinedly never letting go. Never wilfully accepting his fate and the forging of events thereafter. But it's a rough ride to place yourself at odds with reality, and it bore a huge cost. To the people around him, including those he loved. But most of all, I think, to himself. I don't think any of us could truly understand him in this lonely mission, though it was clearly immeasurably important to him, occupied with it as he was to the end. What the mission was exactly, it's hard to say. Perhaps to be the one man who hadn't deserted his father, the one who never left his side.

CHAPTER 12

TERRACED HOUSE TATE

Eric's house, as it was when he lived there, is immortalised on Google Street View. There's a picture taken the year after his mother died. The hedges are a little overgrown. His old Ford Fiesta, with 200,000 miles on the clock, is parked on the front lawn to reduce the insurance.

There's another image taken a few years later. The hedges have been trimmed – by arrangement of my mum. The car has been replaced by a tiny Citroën with just one previous owner, purchased after Eric produced a carrier bag full of banknotes he claimed his mother had left around the house in envelopes.

Then there's a picture taken the year after his death, before the house's new owners had moved in. The hedge is more overgrown than ever, the car gone, the wooden gate ajar. Between the three photographs, the wheelie bins dance around the front yard but one thing stays constant: the net curtain is drawn closed across the window to my uncle's painting room. Even the ripples in the fabric seem to remain undisturbed. There's no clue that behind them lies anything other than an ordinary front room.

Soon after my uncle's funeral, my dad's mind returned to his mission, to the promise he'd made to his brother at the end of his life: to get him an exhibition. Wearily, he announced he would try once again to make contact with the museum. He sounded like he'd lost any real hope of a result and was now just going through the motions. Almost like it had become some abstract ritual.

I felt on the hook for this exhibition too, after the pledge I'd made to my uncle as he lay dying. Call it repayment for all the times he'd picked me up from school in the car with the stained-glass window, and everything else besides. But much more than that, I'd come to really feel his work deserved to be seen. That he was an artist with an interesting story and a rather unique perspective who had created an impressive, committed body of work. I felt he'd earned the right to an exhibition put on by someone who appreciated that. And following that thought, the answer seemed obvious: we should do it ourselves – in his house.

The more I thought about it, the more it made perfect sense. This was the place where we had uncovered all his work, where it had lain hidden from view for decades. This was the place where he had created it all. The idea was partly inspired by the British artist Jeremy Deller. A few years earlier, I'd been to an exhibition of his with a recreation of 'Open Bedroom', an early show Deller had staged in his parents' house while they were away on holiday. 'I decided to . . . turn the slightly embarrassing situation of still living with my mum and dad in my mid-20s into a "feature",' Deller had said. Here Eric could beat Jeremy, having shared his house with his mother until he was seventy-six.

But there was a big difference. In our case, we would be exhibiting a man's life's work – and for the first time.

Doing so without the endorsement of a museum or gallery was a daunting prospect. It seemed a much bigger risk. It would just be us, his family, trying to persuade people that he was worthy of their attention. No institutional seal of approval. We would be fulfilling our promise to him – but only technically. We knew that he had hoped for an exhibition at the local museum. But in the circumstances, there didn't seem much else we could do.

My dad bought the idea, possibly just grateful to be relieved of his futile campaign. But it immediately felt more empowering to be doing something ourselves. There was a new energy to the project. My dad and my aunt agreed to hold off selling the house for a couple of months. A date for the exhibition was chosen – the last weekend in October – which felt like just enough time to prepare everything, but not too long to postpone the serious business of a house sale for a slightly wacky scheme.

On reflection, the date wasn't the most convenient for me. I'd spent most of the year writing and preparing to shoot a Christmas film for the BBC. Filming began a week after our chosen weekend. But it didn't strike me as an issue. It would be nice to have a quiet weekend up north, I thought, before the chaos of a TV shoot. Because I couldn't really imagine who would come to an exhibition in a terraced house in Warrington. I assumed I would spend the weekend sitting on a chair in the corner of my uncle's living room, in the guise of a gallery attendant, as the occasional neighbour or, if we were lucky, local art enthusiast wandered around.

The plan was to open for both days of the weekend with a private view on the Friday, and the private view was the real focus of my scheming – a chance to perhaps lure some art world movers and shakers with the promise of free wine. I had zero experience of putting on art exhibitions but I instinctively felt there must be no expense spared on the wine. In fact, I almost saw the two-day exhibition as the necessary conceptual excuse to host this private view – where maybe, just maybe, someone with some power and influence might take an interest in my uncle's work.

We set about transforming Eric's house into an art gallery.

I had the idea that we would remove all the furniture and carpets, and paint the walls white. Except for two rooms, which would be presented exactly as they were: my uncle's bedroom and his painting room. These seemed to me almost like an extension of his artistic practice and exhibits in themselves. Also to be left untouched were the kitchen, which would be our backstage area, and the bathroom. Our gallery's washroom facilities would have a green shag pile carpet, pink tiles and matching pink fixtures.

My mum's organisational skills and impulses had been a great source of anxiety to Eric, but now they came into their own. She arranged for a house clearance team to remove the furniture and rip up the carpets. And a local painter and decorator was given a brief he'd never received before: to paint all walls, ceilings, skirting, everything, white. 'Like an art gallery.'

I'll confess that we had to somewhat recreate Eric's

painting room. In the final months of his life, when he was living entirely in the back room, the front room had become something of a dumping ground. So I asked my parents if they could restore this, as closely as possible, to its former glory. Over the phone from London, it wasn't always easy to convey my vision for this exhibition. While putting the painting room back together, my mum would sometimes mention to me that they were going to get rid of something – a pile of old newspapers or plastic bags – because the room 'looked like a tip'. And I'd have to persuade her to stop, then try to work out whether this was old tip or new tip, because the tip was part of what people would be coming to see. Then I'd hear my mum sigh down the phone line, concerned about what kind of a show we were putting on here. To the same end, I also tried to persuade her not to get Eric's hedges trimmed – but ultimately failed. It was almost like I had become him.

Meanwhile, I set about taking care of publicity and the all-important invite list for the private view. My approach here was really to try anything – because everything seemed like a long shot. During my lunch hours, I hastily composed a press release: a one-page document explaining how my uncle, Eric Tucker, had left behind hundreds of paintings of working-class life in the industrial north, unseen by anyone outside of immediate family. With the discovery of his work still ongoing, I was editing the details with each day's phone call from my parents. 'Some 200 paintings' became '300 paintings' became 'nearly 400 paintings' in the course of a week – and still an underestimation. I attached some images of my uncle's work and my press release was ready to go. I started at what I considered the top: Will Gompertz, BBC arts editor.

If you were wondering if working as a television scriptwriter helped me at all with my media strategy – if you can call it that – it didn't. I was clueless. Though this might be one, tiny exception. Knowing how BBC email addresses are formatted, I took a punt at Will Gompertz's – and I turned out to be right. Because not two hours after I'd emailed Will, he replied.

My heart was in my mouth as I opened the email.

He began, promisingly, by praising the work. But – he continued, much less promisingly – he wasn't sure he wanted to cover the story. My heart returned to my chest. And then I noticed that he'd rounded off the email by asking if we were planning to sell Eric's work. This slightly blindsided me. With so few straws to grasp at, ending on a question seemed to me like a sliver of hope. But why was Will asking this? Did he want one for his collection? Would it somehow make the story more palatable if we were selling them – or the opposite? I was terrified of putting a foot wrong and perhaps blowing what seemed like an opening, albeit of the very slimmest kind. I decided honesty was the best policy. We hadn't really thought about selling any of the work, I explained. The aim was just to try to get it seen as widely as possible and hopefully generate enough interest for a larger exhibition. I clicked 'send' and hoped for the best.

Next, I began googling the names of every relevant or halfway-relevant curator, conservator, head, assistant head, and acting head of collections and exhibitions, plus the directors and their assistants, at every public art gallery in a fifty-mile radius of my uncle's house, as well as any art critic or correspondent I could find whose curiosity might just conceivably be piqued by this event. I sent them all an invite to our private view.

Five days after I'd emailed Will Gompertz back, and just as I was beginning to give up hope of a reply, he got back to me. He would like to come and film our exhibition. I was ecstatic. We'd done it. I couldn't believe it. In my very first attempt, I'd cracked open the supposedly cliquish art world. I did have a faint sense that, in at least some sections of that world, the BBC's arts editor might be considered not much more of a kingmaker than Tony Hart. But no matter. From where I was standing, we'd hit the jackpot. We were boarding the mothership. I replied to Will, jumping at the offer.

And then . . . silence.

I heard nothing for twelve long days. At which point I sent Will a tentative follow-up email to check if the plan was still afoot. The following day he got back to me, to tell me that it was now looking unlikely due to news coverage being dominated by Brexit. My heart sank. And I wasn't sure who to blame for my disappointment: Will, the BBC or Nigel Farage.

In the meantime, I had received precisely no positive RSVPs to my private view invitations. Just deafening silence, fitfully interrupted by a limp trickle of polite declines. I had also set up a Facebook event and posted it to the pages of various arts groups in the area. Its 'interested' list was languishing at around twenty – most of whom were people I knew. It was a little over a month until the exhibition and it was beginning to look like the world would be very much indifferent to it happening.

The more I looked at my uncle's work, the more I felt it deserved our very best efforts. But I was frightened that these amounted, in reality, to not very much. There was the practical side of this. What did we really know about putting on an exhibition? And there was the fact that it is hard to be an advocate for a relative's artwork. Looking back at the emails I sent imploring people to come to our private view, I noticed how often I would pre-emptively fend off any accusations of familial bias by acknowledging it myself. The effect was somewhat self-defeating. 'Perhaps I'm a little biased,' I would begin, before attempting to make my case as to why I sincerely thought the work was worthy of attention. Ironically, his being my uncle had been a part of why I'd overlooked and failed to investigate his art.

I began to wake in the middle of the night, unable to return to sleep. I feared we were about to spend two days alone in Eric's house, surrounded by his paintings, a small 'Gallery Open' sign sitting pointlessly by his gate; a final, heartbreaking addendum to his life. We would console ourselves by saying that we had done all we could. But really, that would be no consolation at all.

When a relative, whose artwork has no presence in the world, dies and leaves you with hundreds of their paintings – paintings which you know weren't made to pass the time, but are an exposing and deeply held expression of themself and their world – it puts you in a spot. You have no idea how anyone else will respond to the work – if you can even persuade them to look at it at all. You've no idea if there will be a shred of outside interest. You know that, even if you wanted to, you couldn't hold on to it all indefinitely. You would need a house the size of a gallery to display it all. Even just storing it would mean giving up a room or two. And if there was no demonstrable outside interest, what, in the long term, would you be storing it for?

After discovering all of Eric's paintings, and faced with the overwhelming task of clearing his house, my mum had at one point exclaimed, 'We'll have to get a skip!' She hadn't necessarily meant for the paintings, but she hadn't not meant that either. Alongside my worries, her words echoed in my ears as I lay awake in bed. The real dread lurking beneath my fear that nobody might come to the exhibition was what it would mean for the work. I hoped my uncle's paintings would be seen and appreciated as widely as possible but, ultimately, I just hoped they would survive.

October arrived – the month of the show – and with it new hope. I had sent a copy of the press release to the regional TV news programme, *BBC North West Tonight*, and, on the first day of the month, a producer, David, rang me to say they were interested in covering the story. Whether or not they actually would cover it depended on that week's news cycle, he said – a fact that I was now all too aware of. He would call me on the Monday before the exhibition to confirm. And even if they filmed a piece, David stressed, it depended on that day's news as to whether or not it would be broadcast. It sounded tenuous — even the caveat had a caveat — but it was something, at least.

My brother, through his job in retail, knew a guy who worked in public relations. He offered to help us get our press release out. If a newspaper thought it was a good story, they might print it — but, again, there were no guarantees. Still, things seemed to be moving in a more favourable direction. The 'interested' list on my Facebook event was slowly creeping up. But as the week of the exhibition arrived, we had nothing concrete. And crucially, my private view invitations had still not yielded a single positive response.

The week was a busy one for me at work. My co-writer and I had last-minute rewrites of our show to take care of before the imminent start of rehearsals. Even if I'd had the time, there wasn't much more I could do for the exhibition. Meanwhile, at my uncle's house, my dad and his sister had selected and hung the paintings, with practical assistance from my uncle Frank, who invented a system for hanging unframed pictures with electrical tape and wire. At the heart of the exhibition, over the fireplace in the back living room, was my uncle's portrait of his father. Everything was ready to go. All we could do now was sit tight and hope for the best.

The hours ticked by that Monday, but there was no call from David the local news producer. I kept glancing at the time in the top corner of my laptop. Five thirty came and went. I wondered if producers of local news kept office hours. Then at 5.43, an email hit my inbox. It was from him. A reporter and a cameraman would be coming to my uncle's house the following day, he said. That night, I took the last train up to Warrington. I figured this was our one shot at news coverage and I didn't want to leave it to my dad to deal with alone. For his sake – and maybe for the exhibition's. The next morning, the reporter and her cameraman filmed their piece in a whirlwind that carried them back into their van and on to their next story. And I caught a train back to London.

That evening, in north-west England, the story of my uncle's hoard of paintings and his upcoming house exhibition went out at the end of the local BBC news report. With great anticipation, I checked my Facebook event before going to bed. There had been a modest handful of further sign-ups but nothing to write home about.

The following morning, I awoke as I do every day, with my radio alarm clock switching on BBC Radio 4's *Today* programme. Generally, I'll then lie in a sleepy haze for a bit with the news headlines oddly influencing my half-waking dreams – and this day was no exception. I was semi-conscious as the daily review of newspaper stories began and presenter John Humphrys said, in his sprightly Welsh tones, 'The *Mail* and the *Express* both highlight the work of a man dubbed the "Secret Lowry" after a treasure trove of almost four hundred paintings was found at his house when he died in July.' My eyes shot open as adrenaline coursed through my veins. I couldn't quite believe what I was hearing. John continued: 'The *Mail* describes him – Eric Tucker is his name – as a real discovery, and says his evocative images of post-war life in the industrial north share Lowry's mix of warmth and bleakness.' I was now standing on my bed, physically punching the air. Never had I imagined feeling such a visceral rush of warmth and admiration for the *Daily Mail*. And then my jubilation was interrupted. 'Critics believe it [the collection] could be worth hundreds of thousands of pounds,' said John, with the authority of voice that saw him present eighteen years of *Mastermind*. I leapt off the bed and panickingly called my parents.

Sixty of my uncle's paintings were currently hanging on the walls of his vacant house, behind a single cylinder lock on his front door. A flurry of phone calls ensued between me and my parents, my parents and my aunt, my parents and my brother, and my brother and me. When my brother called me he was, by chance, sitting outside my uncle's house in his car. He estimated that a vehicle was slowly driving down the quiet side street, its driver and passengers peering at the house numbers, about every thirty seconds. We deferred to my aunt, a retired probation officer, for what to do next. By the end of the day, we had hired round-the-clock security cover: a guy to be there in the daytime, another to be there at night. In a turn of events I hadn't imagined when I'd gone to bed the previous night, my grandparents' ex-council house now had live-in security guards.

The following day, the rehearsals for my TV show began. I told my seventy-two-year-old mother that I'd have to direct any interview requests to my dad, and therefore to her phone. Because, although my dad has a mobile phone, it is forever out of battery and, when it isn't, he's not great at answering it.

'What should he say to them?' my mum asked, already sounding slightly overwhelmed and hoping, perhaps, that I had some plan here.

'I don't know,' I said with a shrug. 'Just tell them the story.'

On our mid-morning break from rehearsing, I gave her a call to see how they were getting on.

'Your dad's at Radio 5 Live,' she said, sounding mildly spaced out, 'and Sky are going to send a car for him – because I've got ours.'

They had been besieged by requests. Her phone wouldn't stop ringing, she said.

'Joe, what have you done this time?' she said in a low, solemn voice as if I had a history of triggering media circuses.

I was beginning to realise that perhaps I couldn't just leave my pensionable parents to deal with this by themselves – that I'd have to go up north that night. My co-writer, Lloyd, gamely agreed to hold the fort and I made my apologies to the actors and director, explaining that I had an unfolding media situation to deal with. To do with a secret hoard of paintings my late uncle had produced, I added in a slightly garbled fashion, in case they thought I'd committed some heinous crime.

The next day – the day before we opened to the public – the story appeared in a couple more places. But for the most part, the storm had quelled, leaving us time to make the final preparations before the private view that evening. I'd almost entirely failed in my attempts to draw the great and good of the north-west arts scene – with a couple of late exceptions. The previous day, two curators from Warrington Museum and Art Gallery, including the elusive exhibitions officer, plus a curator from Manchester Art Gallery had agreed to come. My mum would fill out the rest of the guest list, she said, with some of my uncle's neighbours, family friends – plus her hairdresser, Pam, and Pam's husband.

My cousins – my aunt's two daughters – and their families arrived to lend a hand. It was emotional for everyone to encounter the house transformed. It had been our grandparents' house; an unchanging fixture in our lives. Even under the sprawling mess of my uncle's sole habitation, it was still recognisably their home. But now we'd stripped them out of it, leaving only him. On top of this, we were seeing his work – the vast majority of it for the first time – exhibited. The walls of the back living room, the hallway, stairs and landing, and two bedrooms were covered in his paintings. They were suddenly out in the light.

My dad arrived. He'd brought with him two hundred copies of an exhibition list he'd painstakingly typed up with his index finger. As my dad's background is in graphic design, they looked great. But we quickly realised there were several discrepancies between the listed titles and the actual paintings on the walls. This was almost too much for him to bear. Who knows what battles, mental and physical, he'd fought to get this Word document typed, formatted and printed. The thought of having to repeat that was more than he could handle. So, with less than an hour before visitors were due to arrive, he began manically removing pictures from the walls – pictures that had been carefully hung according to theme, medium and dimensions – and hastily swapping them for the titles that matched his print-outs. My brother and I tried to stop him. An argument ensued. Voices were raised, expletives used. I could see my mum burning with shame that all this was being witnessed by Raj the security guard.

We managed to persuade my dad to leave the paintings as they were. I would dash to my brother's house, correct the errors and print out a new pile. Taking a copy of the list to mark up the corrections, I noticed that my dad had titled one of the paintings 'Black Man at the Bar'. I told him I didn't think we should call it that. He was incensed, his adrenaline levels still soaring from the discovery of the errors, which he somehow felt was the fault of the computer – of *all* computers. A second argument ensued. I'd gone PC mad. I was expurgating the facts! Look at the painting. Here was a bar, and there was a Black man at it!

With so many paintings on similar themes, titling could be a tricky task. Any quirk or detail that distinguished one painting from the next was liable to form the basis of a title, especially in the bar scenes: 'Titfer and Two Ladies', 'Striped Trousered Gent', 'Mrs Pink Hat with Tot in Hand' are just some of my dad's apt designations. Perhaps I was being overly cautious, with minutes to spare before some curators arrived at the door, but I felt there was something about 'Black Man at the Bar' that failed to capture the spirit of the painting. Of the eight faces visible in the foreground of a hazy midday bar scene, one was a man with dark skin, leaning against the bar.

There was nothing caricatured about him and, other than the colour of his skin, nothing that set him apart from the crowd. He was just depicted as one of the gang.

'Fine,' my dad said with a stressed sigh. 'Call it Jamaican at the Bar.'

We finally agreed on his third suggestion, 'Redhead and Two Bottles of Beer'. Which, of course, I can never quite remember. Unlike 'Black Man at the Bar'.

The next day – Saturday – we opened to the public. I arrived at the house about quarter to nine. It was a clear, crisp autumn morning and I was harbouring a mild hangover, having drunk several glasses of gallery-director-grade wine the night before. All was quiet on King George Crescent. There seemed to be no more cars on the street than usual, no sign of life in the houses, no one about. Then, as I approached the house, a man appeared seemingly from nowhere. He asked me if he was in the right place for the exhibition. He was, I told him, but we didn't open for over an hour. He nodded and wandered off.

I found my parents and my aunt and uncle inside, making cups of tea in our backstage area – the galley kitchen, hidden behind a plastic concertina door. We wondered how many visitors we might expect. There was no way to be sure. The story of Eric's hoard of paintings, along with pictures of his work, had appeared in several newspapers. A few, but not all, of the articles mentioned the exhibition. My Facebook event had seen an increase in activity, but nothing dramatic: by that morning around 180 people had declared themselves 'interested'.

'I think we might get a few more than that,' Frank said, taking a sip of his tea.

I'd bought a wooden A-board on eBay – the kind of thing you see outside a pub advertising Sunday roasts, or outside a coffee shop with a studiedly quirky message. I'd printed posters for each side with the name of the exhibition. We had called it 'Eric Tucker: Sixty Years of Unseen Art' – the earliest exhibited work being one of his sketches from the late 1950s, the latest being an unfinished painting still on his easel when he'd died. I stuck a poster to each side of the board and carried it outside, to be placed on the pavement in front of the house so visitors could spot the gallery.

At around a quarter to ten, I stepped out of the front door. I realised there were people waiting by the front gate. I could see the tops of a few heads peeking over my uncle's newly trimmed privet hedge. I took a few short steps to the rotten front gate and opened it in the required fashion, with a kick to wedge it against the concrete path. I stepped out onto the pavement and found there, to my amazement, a long line of people. I uttered a slightly bewildered 'Morning' as I placed my A-board on the pavement and wandered out into the road. As I backed away from the house, the line opened out to me and I began to see its full span. It ran to the corner of the road and then around it. I wandered along the queue, staring open-mouthed at all the people, none of whom seemed remotely as fazed as me. The line was forty or fifty metres long – with a steady stream of arrivals still joining. There were already several times more people in the queue than we could fit in my uncle's house. In all my worrying, in all my hours of lost sleep, it was the one predicament I had never thought to prepare for: success.

We had to make some hasty practical arrangements. Jobs were doled out between family members plus a couple of friends whose help I called on at the last minute: to be gallery attendants or direct traffic away from the road. We appealed to a nearby pub and a working men's club – both venues my uncle had haunted – to allow us to use their car parks and they kindly obliged. I raced to the nearest printing shop open on a weekend (which wasn't all that near) to order another batch of exhibition handouts. I ordered more than I could imagine us needing. We thought the initial flow of visitors might abate. We were wrong. Thereabouts, the line of people maintained its length for the full two days we were open. I made two further trips to the printers that day, each time ordering a volume I felt sure we couldn't surpass.

My dad had written a short piece on his brother for the handout. It summed Eric up perfectly and more than validated these repeat trips to the printers. A jazz fanatic, my dad had even managed to smuggle in a reference:

> My brother was one of life's irregulars.
> Both ordinary and extraordinary.
> What he did, what he created in his work, he did on his own.
> Little support, little education, certainly no opportunity to go to Art School.
> What he did was to plough his own furrow, to find himself as an artist, unmediated, for good or ill, by any formal training or involvement in the art

establishment and its various movements and cliques over the decades he painted.

He painted from where he stood.

The jazz musician Thelonious Monk wrote 'A genius is the one most like himself'.
My brother in his life and his art was always exactly himself.
He lacked confidence, aspiration and ambition but was also mercifully free of pretence, artfulness and self-aggrandisement in his work.
With little thought or hope of recognition, he painted with total commitment.
He painted because he had to and in doing so conjured a world now lost – with a clarity and consistency that is both painful and joyful.

Over the two days, my dad roamed through the house, chatting to visitors, answering their questions and telling his brother's story. Occasionally, I'd find him backstage in the kitchen, half-dazed on a stool, overwhelmed by it all. After a restorative cup of tea, he'd return re-energised to the fray.

My brother and I took turns outside, controlling the numbers we could fit in the house. We met an eclectic mix of people – people who had travelled from near and far, from around the corner to across the country. There were young and old, families, middle-aged people in Gore-Tex jackets, and nannas with tightly permed hair. There were people who worked in arts administration and education, people who were artists themselves. There were journalists and bloggers, lads in tracksuits, and blokes from down the pub. One lady giddily declared it to be 'like a happening'.

People asked me why my uncle had been so unforthcoming about his art, and what he would have made of all this – two questions I couldn't easily answer. A middle-class South Asian couple mentioned to me, with concern, that they'd read about my uncle using a length of rope for a belt. Were his family not looking after him? I reassured them that my mum had bought him a belt but he had insisted the rope was more practical. They laughed – in a way that suggested they knew the type.

A number of people left the exhibition visibly moved. For many, there was a deeply felt response, my dad noted later, to seeing their lives and their culture as my uncle had depicted them. In seeing them, perhaps for the first time, celebrated. One lady walked out of the house with her headscarf to her mouth, dramatically waving away anyone who might make the mistake of trying to talk to her in that moment. Obsessing over my private view, I had never really considered that we were trying to reach people like this lady – who could have been one of my uncle's characters, or indeed my own grandmother. I hadn't imagined her as the art audience. But here she was, queuing for an art exhibition and leaving it, frankly, more moved than I – an art school graduate – had ever left an exhibition.

Inside the house, people were sure they recognised an old friend or relative in one or other of the paintings. It's possible, though it might rather be testament to Eric's ability to capture character. Some visitors pointed things out to me that I hadn't noticed – like the lady who spotted that one painting depicted an organised dog fight. It was a pleasing but also slightly disconcerting experience. I could feel my uncle shaking his head at my upbringing, one so gilded it had left me unable to recognise a dog fight.

One painting which proved particularly popular was of a coal miner in pitch blackness, looking up towards a shaft of light; a small study, painted on a thick block of wood, and signed and dated 'ERIC 68'. My uncle kept it over the gas fireplace in his painting room. It seemed to stand for the artist himself: a working man, alone in the darkness but looking up to the light. The image is derived from a photograph by Robert Frank of a group of Welsh miners, which appeared in the seminal 1955 exhibition 'The Family of Man' at the Museum of Modern Art in New York. The curator of that exhibition, Edward Steichen, said something of it which seems to me fitting of these two days in my uncle's house: 'The people looked at the pictures, and the people in the pictures looked back at them. They recognised each other.'

As the light began to fade on Sunday, we extended our opening hours. But with the queue still about as long as when we'd opened, we were forced to tell the late joiners that we couldn't admit any more. But we were at least able to assure them that this wouldn't be the last opportunity to see the work of Eric Tucker. Warrington Museum and Art Gallery had confirmed that they would give him a full retrospective. My uncle had his wish.

The final visitor left and we closed the front door. We

gathered together in the back living room, speechless, exhausted and misty-eyed. Me, my parents, my brother, my aunt and uncle, and my cousins. Unprompted, we stood together in a circle and put our arms around one another. The room was filled with a thousand memories for all of us. It was where my dad and my aunt had grown up. Where my brother, my cousins, and I had played countless games of rummy with our grandad. Where I'd spent long hours drawing, watching cartoons and assisting my uncle with his various forms of gambling – shaking the novelty pen that dispensed lottery numbers and marking the 'X' on so many weeks' spot-the-ball entries. It was where we'd argued about Ossie Clark's thumb and fallen about laughing at the foetus that looked like Del Boy Trotter. To these and more, we had added one final unexpected memory: more people had filed through the house in the last forty-eight hours than in the previous forty-eight years. But more importantly, what had seemed far from certain just a few weeks previously now felt possible – that my uncle's work might find a place in the world. As it had transpired, he hadn't needed the endorsement of an institution for the grand unveiling of his life's work. He had drawn the crowds himself.

The following year, Eric's retrospective opened at the town's museum. It was in the run-up to this – the day before opening, in fact – that Alex, the *New York Times* journalist, visited Warrington. Though the house show had been a success, we still felt a great deal of trepidation at this point. This is what we had been building towards.

This was the exhibition my uncle had really wanted. Would interest in his work have sustained, we wondered. Would this exhibition draw enough people to validate a show at a public gallery? The call from Alex, in the week we opened, seemed like a bad omen. But doubts were quickly dispelled. Eric's exhibition soon became one of the most popular in the museum's 170-year history.

Midway through its run, a producer for National Public Radio in the US got in touch. A journalist came to cover the story and, a few weeks later, I awoke one morning to a deluge of emails from listeners across the United States. My uncle had made it across the Atlantic after all. A number of the emailers mentioned the name of their hometown – places in all corners of the US, most of which I'd never heard of. Turns out there are a lot of Warringtons out there.

At the end of the exhibition's run, I met with two London galleries – the sort that sell Post-Impressionist paintings in ornate frames to serious collectors. The year after the retrospective at the museum, they jointly put on a show of Eric's work – in Cork Street, London's famous address for galleries in the shadow of the Royal Academy; the same windows my uncle had peered into after he'd gone to collect his rejected painting all those years ago. The exhibition proved to be the fastest-selling in either gallery's history. Critics described his work as 'serious stuff', 'a remarkable, important find', and 'an incredible coup for British art'. Nobody was more astonished than those of us who had known him. The impossible had happened. Eric Tucker was a glittering success.

* * *

Of course, all of this is bittersweet. Because my uncle lived to see absolutely none of it. It's a regret that my family and I have shared at every turn. Tempered, I must admit, by a strong inclination that likely none of it could have happened – would have been allowed to happen – if my uncle were alive.

Even if I'd managed to persuade him of the idea of the house show – which I'm sure I wouldn't have, especially if I'd started saying things like 'Jeremy Deller' – it's all too easy to imagine him pulling the plug at the eleventh hour. Likewise if my dad had secured the museum exhibition. Something would have halted it as we got into the details. There'd be a casual mention, one day, that he'd decided against it, a decision both inscrutable and immovable.

It's unfortunate because I think he would have delighted in seeing how his work has been received. Though it clearly wasn't what motivated him, I've come to believe he did want his paintings to be seen and appreciated. But in his lifetime, for so many reasons, it was an equation too complex to solve.

As an ending, it seems to frame my uncle as an ultimately tragic character. Which in many ways, he was. But this might be his final contradiction. Because he appeared, on the whole, very content. He was both devoid of self-confidence and the person with the surest sense of himself that I have ever met.

That fact really hit me at his funeral. It was something my dad mentioned in the eulogy he gave for his brother. And perhaps it was accentuated by the fact that, usually in a eulogy, you might hear mention of children, grandchildren, a spouse, perhaps career achievements – and, of course, my uncle had none of these. My dad recalled a moment when they'd been standing together, one warm summer's day, on the coastal path in Pembrokeshire, during one of our family holidays. Looking out across the clear, calm sea, his brother had turned to him and said, 'It's a wonderful world, Tony.' And that was, basically, how he saw things. It's a great place out there. Especially around the rougher edges.

I wondered where he had found this contentment. I thought about the fact that, among all his posthumous successes, the most emotional moment for me – the thing that felt like the greatest victory of them all – was when I realised just how much work he had produced. Those days when my parents rang to tell me they'd found yet another stash of paintings in his house. And then when I finally saw them all. Not the amount so much as the fact he'd done it. Why was that?

I thought back to the dream he shared with his workmate, Brian, sixty years earlier: to go to St Ives and be a painter. It had struck me, at first, as very much a dream unrealised. He hadn't gotten anywhere near St Ives – the place, or the life it implied. But then I thought about it again. I was touched by the fact that it wasn't a dream based in personal glory – to find fame and fortune or win a prize – but simply the dream to live as an artist. And I realised that, in spite of so much, he had lived the life of an artist. He did achieve his dream.

POSTSCRIPT

The origins of this book go back earlier than I first realised. They predate the unearthing of my uncle's work. The first seed was planted that Sunday, as a teenager, when I filmed him telling his stories. That whole project was really an excuse to get Eric and his tales on tape. Newly in possession of a camcorder, I had an urgent sense that both needed to be recorded.

Years later, when Eric was living alone in the back room of his house, I thought again about filming him – to make a documentary. Partly I was thinking of the artist Richard Billingham's work; scenes in my uncle's house were increasingly reminiscent of Billingham's photographs of his parents' squalid flat. Partly I thought there was something Herzogian about Eric's mission to remain in his home – a one-man battle with destiny that seemed bound to end in chaos and collapse.

The thought bubbled away alongside other ideas that never made it to fruition. I knew I'd regret not having filmed him but, at the same time, I knew the reality of filming would be awkward. If he would even allow it. He would likely be suspicious – and not unjustly. It might feel like I was making a spectacle of him. It wasn't the time or the way to tell his story. But still there was that urge that he must be captured. That he was too extraordinary to go undocumented. And yet at the same time, representative of thousands of men whose lives go largely unchronicled in fact or fiction.

That feeling was a large part of my motivation to write this book. And of course, I hoped that telling Eric's story might help raise his profile as an artist and bring attention to his work. On that front, as his nephew, I didn't necessarily feel like the best person for the job. Writing about artists can often exalt and mystify them – it's hard to do that about someone who picked you up from school, someone you've filled in spot-the-ball competitions with and witnessed stealing sachets of sugar. A book written by someone more removed might better supplement his work. But I also had the feeling, given Eric's character and his idiosyncratic journey as an artist, that it might not. How could you really write a straightforward biography of my uncle as an artist anyway? In one way, his life and his art were deeply entwined, but in another, when it came to the actual events of his life, they were very separate: the artist in him largely hidden, his art-making mostly private.

With his profile as an artist in mind, I sometimes worried about the humorous content of this book. Would it undermine efforts to have his work taken seriously? But in those moments, I turned to his paintings for guidance – which can be humorous, though they're never only that. He saw that people and life can be ridiculous and frequently depicted them as such, regardless of how it might affect the status of his work. He seemed to know that concepts of highbrow and lowbrow, though they're very often things people are interminably concerned with, are completely flimsy compared to the real virtues of art. The best account of Eric Tucker, I thought, was one which could take him seriously – and also not. I could give that account, as he had of the people he painted.

I hadn't always been an advocate for my uncle's art. Far from it. As a relative, there's perhaps an assumption of familial bias, that of course you're a fan. But actually, I think the opposite tends to be true – you're more likely to overlook a family member's achievements and fail to consider them special, or at least something beyond what they are to you.

Certainly, that's where my relationship with my uncle's work began: disinterest. The relatively small number of his paintings I'd seen when I was young – mostly the few my parents owned – I was so familiar with, they were like wallpaper. There was a degree of recognition of the skill level – in the earlier paintings at least, which were more realist in style. It seemed like he'd slacked off a bit since then. But even there, it felt difficult to fully attribute this to the man I knew.

I wasn't much moved by the subject matter either. I couldn't really understand why he wanted to paint backstreets and pubs. And his characters seemed extinct to me, based on some distant memory, or perhaps just made up. Though the one occasion I saw him draw in a pub, when he took me with him one day during the school holidays, prompted a flicker of reappraisal. I watched as he slipped a sketch pad out of his jacket and surveyed the bar. I noticed the people he selected and the way he saw them, and I realised that they were indeed his characters. I had the faintest sense that perhaps he was doing something I hadn't appreciated. But it wasn't enough to shift my opinion.

In my teenage years, I felt slightly embarrassed about his paintings, inasmuch as I ever thought about them at all. I would've preferred they were more modern, abstract or inscrutable. They weren't exactly to my informed and discerning tastes, I thought, having recently heard of the YBAs. Even the pride I felt at his purchase by the museum was tempered by the fact that the painting included a Yates's Wine Lodge – which now seems to me like a brilliant decision. Dreadfully, at the same time, I was swanning around school in his labourer's donkey jacket.

Shortly after Eric's death, a discovery brought home to me how knowing a person too well can cloud your view. The story begins a decade earlier when my uncle claimed that some of his paintings had been stolen from his front room. Firemen had called at his house – they were going down the street, fitting free smoke alarms. He had tried to put them off but, to his horror, they had gone into his painting room. And to be fair, if ever a room was in need of a fire safety intervention, that was it – with its piles of books, crisply aged newspapers, and turpentine-soaked rags. They fitted the alarm, but Eric believed they had made off with several paintings. Shamefully, we didn't really believe him. Half-entertaining the possibility, we wondered if they could have been thieves posing as firemen, but enquiries confirmed that, no, this was indeed a visit by the local fire service. So it seemed to us like Eric's usual paranoia had been sent into overdrive by, understandably, having hated feeling out of control of the situation. Why, we thought, would firemen be interested in his paintings?

Then, following his death, when we opened his house as a gallery, a man turned up with a painting – a painting that my dad felt certain he'd seen in his brother's front room years earlier. The man had bought the work at an auction, not long after Eric claimed he'd had pictures stolen. We realised his suspicions were correct. The thieves had seen value in his work where we had failed to.

It was only after my uncle's death, once I realised just how much work he'd produced, that I really began to look at it. I asked my dad when he had first seriously appreciated his brother's abilities as a painter. It was the same moment, he told me, sounding regretful. Perhaps a part of this was because Eric, along with his self-image, had left the picture. But most of all, the sheer volume of work demanded proper attention. That he had produced it with little thought of recognition underlined the fact: he had really meant this.

I immediately felt there was something amazing about the collection, something pretty rare and unique. The work was certainly interesting. Many have created art, in different mediums, about working-class communities or 'ordinary life' more broadly, but few have done it from a perspective so close and involved as his. And perhaps partly because it had been produced so hermetically, the work felt extraordinarily personal. I began to feel that some of it was good – that some of it was very good. Even then, I had a mountain of junk to remove before I could see his achievements clearly. I mean that metaphorically, but it was also sometimes literally true.

I wondered if he was an outsider artist because it was the bracket I thought he might fit into. (It isn't necessarily a wrong label for him, and though it might have its problems, it does at least acknowledge that there is a set of conventions that some artists are outside of.) But I realise now that I was also trying to find a context which was more comfortable for me. It took me a little while until I was able to view the work on its own terms – to reconcile my own issues with it being, in different ways, both sophisticated and not. Other people's reactions to it helped get me there.

I became much more familiar with Eric's paintings through cataloguing them and helping to organise exhibitions. I came to appreciate how carefully he'd composed his scenes and formulated his colour schemes. How he'd used texture and contrast. I saw how he'd mastered his medium, achieving in it, it seems, exactly what he wanted to, and an absolute sense of himself on the canvas.

Still his paintings would surprise me. Something that had come out from under his bed, that I'd looked at a dozen times by then, would get framed and hung on a gallery wall, and only then would I really see it and appreciate what he'd done.

I began to appreciate how he'd done it, and to think about why. That's when the memory came back to me of watching him pick out and sketch characters I had thought no longer existed. I came to feel that time was significant in his work. Art is usually preoccupied with the new but, working in his own vacuum, my uncle seemed determined to show that the past is still with us. Certainly it was for him. In many of his scenes, time feels ambiguous. The fact that he very rarely saw any point in dating his pictures seems to add to that. Even when he's most obviously painting the past, I don't think it's simple nostalgia or social record. He is still partly there. So, it seems, are many of his characters.

Ultimately, I realised that even when I'd started to take notice of my uncle's work, I'd still hardly taken it in. In fact, I began to appreciate that I'd hardly looked at paintings generally – not compared to him. This was, frankly, embarrassing. Because I was forty, and a card-carrying Tate member with an art school degree. I hadn't imagined that my uncle could teach me anything. Which meant I hadn't imagined he could show me anything.

My uncle's work changed me and, likewise, the experience of exhibiting it changed my perspective on who the 'art audience' is. Asked to describe it, I suppose I'd have pictured the sort of people Grayson Perry might lightly satirise in a tapestry. But the visitors to the exhibition at my uncle's house, and the museum a year later, were incredibly diverse. Invariably, my focus was on the middle-class people – the visitors who did look a bit like Grayson Perry characters. Because I felt that they would surely be the ones to somehow manifest future exhibitions of my uncle's work. And the ugly fact is that's probably true. But many of those most moved by the work were, of course, working-class people – people very much like my uncle's characters, who didn't necessarily look like committed gallery-goers. I mentioned the lady who walked out of the house show with her scarf to her mouth. Truthfully, I had found it quite funny at the time. It was only later that it occurred to me I'd never left an exhibition so moved – the joke was on me. As my uncle had been a hidden painter, she was a hidden art fan. As his ambitions were unnourished to the point of near-invisibility, so, it seems, was her appreciation.

The nineteenth-century designer William Morris said, 'I do not want art for a few, any more than education for a few, or freedom for a few.' One hundred and fifty years later, it still feels like a point in need of being made. In initiatives to open up the arts, social class tends to be neglected compared to the equally worthy causes of other underrepresented groups. And so far, there hasn't been any great concerted effort to posthumously better recognise such artists.

My uncle could be said to be a surprise late entry to the 'Northern School' – a loosely connected group of modern British artists mostly defined and championed by enthusiasts and dealers, rather than curators and public galleries. It includes painters like Theodore Major, Alan Lowndes and Sheila Fell – all highly celebrated in their time, but since largely neglected. The north, it could be argued, has been as inspirational a landscape to artists as the Cornish coast, but its interpreters don't enjoy anything like the legacy of the twentieth-century St Ives artists.

Beyond this, Eric is part of an even more loosely defined and underexposed group: working-class artists making art about the experience of working-class life. The enormous popularity of Lowry surely at least partly reflects a great, and perhaps underserved, public appetite to see that world and that experience – an integral part of our national identity and story – depicted. Though ironically, Lowry was something of an outsider to this experience – it's often been said that his work conveys the feeling of loneliness in a crowd.

In a book about someone like my uncle, it would be an oversight not to at least touch on systemic unfairness and exclusion. It's important to acknowledge. But I'm also aware that, for those who feel at a disadvantage when it comes to pursuing creative work, these facts can feel dispiriting. What's the point in trying? My final reason for telling Eric Tucker's story – and I suppose this isn't unrelated to raising the profile of his work – is that I hope it can inspire others, especially those who feel some kinship with him. Of course, I wouldn't recommend taking my uncle's attitude of being possessive and secretive about your endeavours. But to me, his great victory was that, to a world that told him in innumerable ways that he couldn't be an artist, he proved that he was and that he couldn't not be. By doing the work, with unwavering commitment.

In the end, he made, by any measure, a pretty sensational posthumous debut. He proved that his work could draw crowds and win critical plaudits. But now is really the crucial test of whether he will achieve any kind of ongoing legacy. And it's hard not to have the sense of a working-class mother telling her son he'll have to work ten times as hard as the other boys. I hope there will be future exhibitions of Eric Tucker's work. I think the best of it deserves to be held in public collections. I hope the end of this book isn't the end of the story but, for his art, and for other artists like him, just the beginning.

ACKNOWLEDGEMENTS

I'd like to first of all thank everyone who spoke to me about my uncle for this book, most of all my dad, my aunt and my brother for sharing their memories, and my mum for filling in the gaps. Also, a second shout out to my dad for allowing me to include his written piece on his brother without even a mention of copyright infringement or payment.

Beyond this, I'd like to thank everyone who appears in the book. I think everyone included in this story in some way helped better shape my understanding of my uncle and his work – though so have many others who aren't included – and I'm very grateful to all who have engaged with Eric's work and story.

Thanks to Ruth Millington for persuading me to start. To Lloyd Woolf for being accommodating and for submitting to my Eric anecdotes – some of the thoughts in Chapter 10 came out of our discussions and Lloyd's wisdom fed into them. Thanks also to Liam Iandoli for his help and cheerleading. To Victoria Manifold for being the first reader. And a big thanks to Kath Simpson for all her support and enthusiasm, for giving me my 'why', and helping to keep the train moving.

Special thanks to Jane Finigan at Lutyens & Rubinstein for having faith in this story, helping shape it into a book and finding it a great home. To Abby Singer at Casarotto Ramsay for being an all-round amazing agent and human. To Simon Thorogood at Canongate for taking the punt, providing cool-headed guidance and incisive snips. To Jamie Byng, Leila Cruickshank, Amaani Banharally, Jamie Norman and everyone else at Canongate who gave the book their support and energies. And to Robert Sharman for making me look like a better writer.

For their parts in giving this story its ending, thanks to Ed Watson, and to Janice Hayes, Roger Jeffrey, Craig Sherwood and all at Warrington Museum & Art Gallery and Culture Warrington, and to Alon Zakaim, Ben Springett and all at Alon Zakaim Fine Art, and Anthony Brown and all at Connaught Brown. I beg forgiveness from the good people of Warrington for my impressions of growing up there. Your hometown is like your family – you're allowed to make fun, but nobody else better try it. And in answer to those who called it Britain's worst town for culture, my uncle, I know, would say: rubbish. There's more culture to be found in one pub in the town than a dozen listed buildings. Also, have they been to Widnes?